Street and Place Names in Watford

Below: a charming sketch map from the Watford Terrier
of 1798

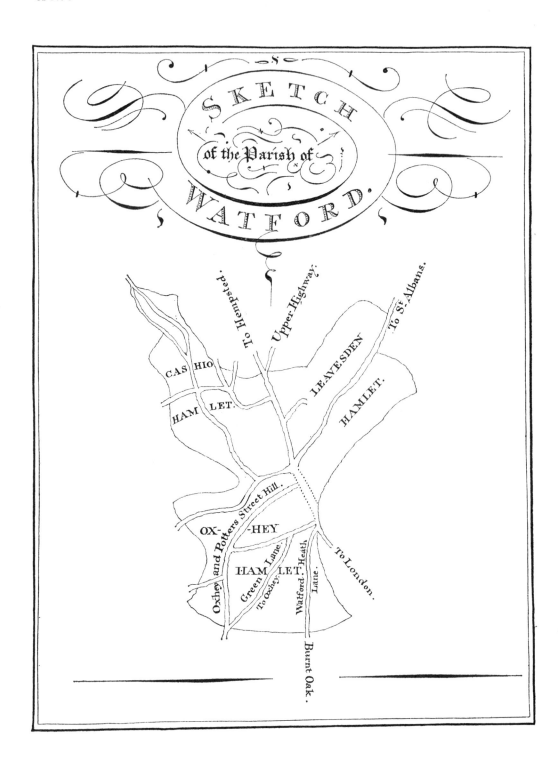

Alan W. Ball B.A., F.L.A.
BOROUGH LIBRARIAN

Street and Place Names in Watford

PUBLISHED BY
WATFORD BOROUGH COUNCIL
1973

THE BOROUGH ARMS

In the top third of the shield are the Arms of St. Albans to commemorate the long association between that city and Watford. The 'harts' represent the Herts in Hertfordshire.

In the lower part of the shield occur two escallop shells taken from the Arms of the Earl of Clarendon, Charter Mayor. The wavy blue and white lines represent the ford in Watford.

The fasces in the centre denote magisterial authority.

The motto 'Audentior' is a quotation from Virgil's *Aeneid* VI, 95: 'tu ne cede malis, sed contra *audentior* ito, quam tua te Fortuna sinet'. (Yield not thou to ills, but go forth to face them *more boldly* than thy Fortune shall allow thee.)

© Alan W. Ball, 1973
ISBN   0 903408 02 3   (Cloth)
ISBN   0 903408 03 1   (Paperback)
Printed in Great Britain by Sun Printers Ltd., London and Watford

ACKNOWLEDGEMENTS

Inevitably, in a work of this kind a great deal depends on the help and co-operation of other people. I would therefore like to thank most warmly all the following people for a great deal of information and sound advice:

Mr. Herbert Rolfe, a former Borough Councillor, Mr. Frederic Vince, a past Mayor of Watford and an estate agent in the town over a long period of time, Mr. John Weller, also an estate agent for many years, Mr. Cecil Judge, at one time a local builder, and both the Town Clerk and Chief Executive Officer, Mr. Gordon Hall, and the Director of Technical Services, Mr. Richard Brand, with many members of their respective staffs. In addition, I have had the privilege of using notes left by my predecessor in office, Mr. Robert Sayell. Mr. Howard Colvin of St. John's College, Oxford, made valuable suggestions about the possible origins of Watford Place, while special thanks must go to Mr. Leonard Johnson, also a former Mayor of the Borough and at one time Archivist to the British Transport Commission, and Alderman Hubert Buckingham. As well as making proposals for improvements, they carried out the onerous task of reading the whole work in proof. Two members of my own staff deserve a special mention. Mr. Ronald Codlin, the North Watford Branch Librarian and a lifelong Watfordian, and Miss Margaret Marshall, the Reference Librarian. Both drew my attention to a great deal of material, which I would have otherwise missed, and also cast sceptical eyes over some of my wilder theories. Miss Marshall also read the whole work in proof.

Finally it gives me the greatest pleasure in thanking my wife for her professional advice as an architectural historian, which has made my task a great deal easier than it would otherwise have been.

CONTENTS

ILLUSTRATIONS

INTRODUCTION

Until the second half of the nineteenth century, Watford[1] was a small south midland market town with the Great Wen of London, that William Cobbett loathed so much, merely a rather unfortunate excrescence on the distant skyline. It is true that the Grand Junction Canal[2] had been built in the late eighteenth century, but its newness soon mellowed and became part of the landscape, as if it had been there from time immemorial. Even the snorting monster of the railway was kept at arm's length when it first appeared in 1837, as the Earl of Essex and the Earl of Clarendon between them had so much influence, that they were able to prevent it crossing their Estates[3] at Cassiobury and the Grove. This caused vast extra expense in engineering works, as a wide detour around the town had to be made. If the Grand Junction Canal had not been developed along the present route from Rickmansworth to Hunton Bridge, but had followed more closely the line of the River Colne, it is possible that Watford could have become an interchange point between water and rail. Although canal receipts fell dramatically at the coming of the railways, this was not the result of less tonnage being carried, but was caused by a drastic reduction in charges to meet the new competition. It is therefore clear that sufficient business would have remained to make an appreciable impact on the life of the town and this co-ordination of transport facilities might well have accelerated the growth of housing and commerce generally.[4] It was not until well over a century later in 1963 that the greatly enlarged freight terminal at Watford Junction brought about transport co-ordination, but by this time of course it was between road and rail. The whole process may however soon turn full circle, as there is a current suggestion that a large new interchange area between the M.1. and the Grand Union Canal might be created at Berkhamsted. This is because the road system in the area has become so congested that the Canal may well offer a better means for certain heavy goods to be transported to the London Docks[5]. Some charming buildings that pre-date the advent of the railway still remain in the town. The earliest of these is the partially thirteenth century parish church of St. Mary and the earliest inhabited dwellings are the Bedford Almshouses of 1580. Monmouth House was built in the early seventeenth century and extensively restored and altered in 1927 when the ground floor was made into shops. Little Cassiobury, possibly the best classical house in Watford, is of the late seventeenth century and was at one time a dower house for the Cassiobury Estate. The Free School dates from 1704 and Frogmore House and Russells from 1718. This latter was also a dower house for the Cassiobury Estate, but at an earlier date than

Little Cassiobury, although it is of course the later of the two buildings. Also of eighteenth century construction is the former home of the Dyson and Benskin families, which is now used as offices for the Cannon Brewery. The Grove was built in 1756 by Sir Robert Taylor to replace an existing house, enlarged in 1780 by Matthew Brettingham and altered again in 1850. The property was the home of the Villiers family (created Earls of Clarendon in 1776) from 1753 until 1935, the period between 1753 and 1756 being spent in the former house. In 1939 it was acquired by the London, Midland and Scottish Railway and now serves as a productivity services training centre for the British Railways Board.

In addition, special mention should be made of Watford Place, constructed or rebuilt about 1825. This simple but dignified house looks as if it were designed by an architect rather than merely being the work of a local builder.[6] The only other edifice that should be noted before 1850 is the former Workhouse, which replaced, if this were possible, even more insalubrious premises. It is an undistinguished, hard-as-nails, no-nonsense building of 1838 by an architect, presumably a local man, named Weedon. It has an entrance porch like a sentry box and an air of gloom abounding, the very epitome of what the Victorians delighted in producing for institutions of this kind. In common with a multitude of other workhouses through-out the country, it proved to be a useful reach-me-down for the care of the sick and was incorporated into Shrodells Hospital, where it is now dominated mercifully by a new maternity block designed by Fred Maunder, Regional Architect of the North West Metropolitan Regional Hospital Board.

The period from 1830 to 1850 was a difficult one economically for this country and the 1840's saw only a very small amount of building in Watford. This was at Carey Place, Grove Circus and around the railway station, then on the St. Albans Road. Thus by 1849 the town had hardly expanded beyond its original nucleus as the following description makes clear:

'Watford is composed of a principal street, about $1\frac{1}{2}$ miles long, built upon a sort of ridge sloping southwards to the river. On either side and communicating with this street are numerous courts and alleys, composed of small tenements, in which the bulk of the population is lodged. There are scarcely any cross streets and the town is nowhere above 440 yards, and seldom above 220 yards broad. The London and Birmingham Railway passes about a mile from the top of the town. About the station and along the road leading to it from Watford, houses have recently been built and are still in progress'.[7]

The Nascot or Nascot Wood estate north and west of Langley Road owes its development as a pleasant residential area from the 1850's onwards in large measure to the proximity of the railway, as householders were offered preferential rates of travel if they commuted to London. In the High Street area new housing and business premises were first developed on a really planned basis in 1851 with the opening of King Street, but a project to push this across the line of the present Vicarage Road came to nothing. 1860 saw the beginning of Queen's Road (often called Queen Street) and Clarendon Road followed in 1864, although at the publica-tion of the 1871 25-inch Ordnance Survey Map, the development of the area between the High Street and the Junction Station was by no means completed.

Alexandra Road, Denmark Street and Essex and Malden Roads on the west side of the St. Albans Road had only just been laid out, but still had no houses, although the first two had been named in honour of the Danish Princess Alexandra's wedding to the Prince of Wales in 1863, an event which gave rise to great festivities in the town. At the same time the then independent village of Oxhey started to grow and it is a fact now too little appreciated, that on a sale plan of 1857, Capell, Paddock and Villiers Roads were all named and had started to develop before Queen's and Clarendon Roads. In addition, the area around Watford Heath formed a tiny hamlet in its own right by the eighteenth century or even earlier. By 1842 there were about sixteen cottages and in 1866 these had increased to twenty-eight with a public house to cater for the expanding clientele.

Nearer the centre of the town the period after 1860 produced two charitable buildings that deserve attention, the Salters' Company Almshouses in Church Road and the London Orphan Asylum (now occupied as offices by the Department of Employment) in Orphanage Road. The former is of 1864 in a neo-Tudor style by Thomas Charles Sorby with decorative iron gates to the street and large cedar trees giving a delightfully spacious air.[8] The latter of 1871 is in a faceless Gothic style by Henry Dawson, which its original inhabitants must have found cold and cheerless and time has not softened in the slightest.[9]

Public utilities were slow in being introduced and it was not until 1834, more than a quarter of a century after Pall Mall was lit by gas in 1808, that this advance appeared in Watford. In 1854 the first waterworks was built, not because this was considered a progressive move, but in rather unseemly haste as the result of a cholera outbreak.

After 1850 the newly formed Local Board of Health started to grapple with the insanitary conditions that prevailed. Arrangements for the disposal of refuse and sewage were of the most elementary kind and as fast as one nuisance was dealt with, several others sprang up to take its place. The following description shows not only the wretchedness of conditions generally, but also highlights the haphazard building practices of the time, which helped to create a formidable public health problem: "At the Post Office, a newly erected building, the garden slopes towards and drains upon the house. The drainage of the back yard is led into the street by an iron pipe, laid between the ceiling of the kitchen and the floor of the room above. In this house last year seven children were all attacked with fever, and three died. Mr. Smith, Surgeon, states, 'I am of the opinion the disease was produced, and the symptoms rendered more severe in consequence of bad drainage, so that the filth was coming into the cellar through the wall.' Red-Lion-Yard, Boot and Pump-Yards (both fever localities), and Water Lane, contain pigsties, dung-heaps, privies, overflowing cesspools, dirty gardens and badly paved passages".[10]

In these circumstances it is not surprising to find the life of the Board's officials difficult in the extreme, as they tried to come to terms with a populace that violently resented their attentions. Butchers regularly left mounds of the more unsaleable parts of their stock in trade to decay in the streets and a sturdy independence, still deeply rooted in a recent agricultural past, meant that there was much illicit keeping of pigs, rabbits and other livestock, as the following entries from the log-

book of two of these officials make abundantly clear.[11] Although the writing lacks a certain literary quality, it more than compensates for this deficiency by the forthright manner of its presentation:

'September 4th 1853. Cautioned Mr. Maddon for allowing his cart to be washed at the Pond. If continued, a summons would be applied for.

October 6th 1853. Cautioned Jas. Selwood for keeping pigs and told his wife that they must be removed immediately: near the Rail Road Station.

April 7th 1855. Cautioned Hollingsworth, Butcher, not to allow offal and dung to accumulate or to remain as it is at present near the roadside—Pump Meadow, Water Lane and immediately opposite Lucy Deacon's. He said he should have it taken there, the Board may do what they liked.

October 20th 1856. Complaints of a dreadful stench near the Turnpike near Bushey Station. I find it arises through the gully being connected with the sewer without a proper trap, and several closets being connected with the sewer at that end causes it to be very offensive'.

There can be no more eloquent testimonial to the steady progress of local government over one hundred and twenty years than a comparison between the squalor described above and conditions prevailing today. It is a sobering thought, that if small market towns like Watford could be described in this way, sense almost faints picturing the conditions that prevailed in London and the large industrial cities of the Midlands and the North.

Although Watford does not have any of the really great features of early railway engineering, railwaymen have always lived in the town since the opening of the line. A locomotive suburban depot was established in 1890 and with the availability of housing in the Callowland area of North Watford a few years later the population of railway workers increased rapidly.

To stand today on one of the platforms at Watford Junction and to see the whispering electric trains burst upon the station, batter it with great waves of sound and as quickly depart, is to feel again the thrill of the early pioneering days of steam locomotion and to sense that here is a formerly slumbering giant, which at one time was yielding ground steadily to the apparently inexorable advance of the triumphant internal combustion engine, suddenly awakening to a new and inspiring existence. There is once more the urgency of swift travel to the industrial cities of the Midlands and the North with average running times becoming steadily less and less, nowhere more vividly illustrated than just east of Daventry, where the railway, the Grand Union Canal and the M.1. come together and the railway traveller can watch motorists doing seventy in the fast lane gradually slip backwards out of sight.

One of the most significant elements in the development of the town from the 1870's until the First World War was the amount of building carried out by William Gough. He was born at Aynho in Northamptonshire and came south to Watford, where he was to join up with Edwin Clifford to form in 1868 the still existing firm of Clifford and Gough. The fact that he was born in Aynho and spent his boyhood in that immediate area, meant that many South Northamptonshire and North Oxfordshire names were used not only for streets, but also for groups of houses

within streets. As the firm also worked as monumental masons, he designed a distinctive plaque with scrolls and foliage to carry these names and in addition used other, plainer, styles extensively.[12]

His preference was for yellow stock brick with straight bands, geometric designs and sometimes dates picked out in red brick. The houses he built were almost exclusively two storey and of the type commonly found in small midland towns, which he would have known so well. They are in marked visual contrast to the style of housing being erected in London at that time, which was often of three storeys, and the traveller from the South, sensitive to such things, realises at once on entering Watford, that he has come to one of those regional boundaries, which even in twentieth century England are almost as marked as ever.[13] Until the growth of the large national brick companies, the stock bricks used in the town came mainly from two local brickyards, one at Leverstock Green and the other in Lower Paddock Road.

The sale of the Holywell, Harwoods, Bradshaw and Callowland Estates in the 1880's and 1890's released a great deal of land for development in the late Victorian and Edwardian period. This produced a three-fold jump in population from just over ten thousand in 1881 to almost thirty thousand by 1901, and this process was repeated after the First World War when Cassiobury House and Park and also land north of Gammon's Lane came onto the market and this again increased the population to nearly fifty-seven thousand by 1931.

One highly ambitious Edwardian project that never materialised was the 'New Town' estate of 1908.[14] It would have been a logical extension of the Nascot Wood estate and the promoters issued a large and imposing prospectus in which the following details of the proposed scheme were given:

'50 valuable freehold building sites, being the first portion of the New Town Estate, having extensive frontages to the above roads and proposed roads with long depths, the sites of half an acre, well suited for the erection of picturesque villas, country cottages, shops and business premises, which are in demand in this growing locality.'

The land was eventually bought for £27,500 following the First World War by the Urban District Council, which developed the area as the Harebreaks estate.[15] The consultant architect was E. Vincent Harris and the main contractor was Charles Brightman. In layout the estate is an early example of others that followed in the London area such as the Becontree estate in Dagenham, the Watling estate in Hendon, the Westway estate in Hammersmith, the St. Helier estate in Morden and the Downham estate in Lewisham.

Before proceeding to consider in more detail the architecture of the inter-war and post-war periods, it would seem appropriate at this juncture to look at the more outstanding ecclesiastical buildings of the town. Apart from the medieval parish church of St. Mary there is a complete gap until 1853 when All Saints, Leavesden, was built. Thus there are none of the elegant Georgian and Regency churches or even any early non-conformist chapels, that in many towns produce such a pleasing architectural continuity through the centuries from the Middle Ages to the present day. In this way a complete vacuum was left, which the Victorians with their

delight in architectural styles of many preceding periods were only too happy to fill. It would have been surprising indeed if the indefatigable Sir George Gilbert Scott, that great builder and renovator of churches, had not set foot in Watford. He was in fact responsible for All Saints, Leavesden, where he did a very workman-like job in his best tradition, while he was also commissioned to carry out fairly extensive alterations to St. Mary's in 1848.

St. Andrew's, Church Road, which has strong associations with the railway, as many railwaymen lived in the parish, was designed in 1857 by Sebastian Sanders Teulon.[16] For an architect, who was a kind of Victorian neo-brutalist given to aggressively ugly buildings with a surfeit of polychrome brickwork, it is a remark-ably discreet work. The genesis of St. John's, Sutton Road, provides an interesting sidelight on the attitudes of the day. During the second restoration of St. Mary's in 1871 a tin tabernacle was erected nearby to provide accommodation for the congregation while re-building was in progress. After this work was completed, the tin tabernacle naturally became surplus to requirements and the Anglican authorities had it transported to Sutton Road until a permanent structure was built in 1893. Thus they were able to combine very neatly three interests dear to the Victorian heart, piety, economy and a fascination with prefabrication first aroused by the Crystal Palace, which Joseph Paxton had erected in Hyde Park to house the Great Exhibition of 1851.

Holy Rood Roman Catholic Church of 1890 in Market Street, one of the best examples of late Victorian Gothic, is the work of John Francis Bentley, who among many other commissions designed Westminster Cathedral. By a subtle piece of ecclesiastical one-upmanship, which gently but firmly emphasised a tradition with a much longer continuity, the top of the spirelet was made to reach three feet nearer to God than that of St. Mary's. The most noteworthy contribution of nonconformity is the Beechen Grove Baptist Church of 1878 by J. Wallis Chapman. This is in an Italianate style with an apse towards Clarendon Road and an attached campanile with a pyramid roof, and the whole building would not look out of place on the banks of the Arno.

The public houses of the town are almost all Victorian or later and even those like the Hit and Miss which have parts of their premises dating back to the sixteenth, seventeenth or eighteenth centuries, have been so altered since their original build-ing, that the new far outweighs the old. This is also true of some of the smaller shops in the High Street, especially those at the lower end, although a surprising amount of timber framing often remains behind present-day facades.

The principal local builders in the first two decades of the twentieth century were Clifford & Gough, William Judge, William King, C. & J. Waterman, Bracey & Clarke, Charles Brightman and William Ashby. The latter two also continued to build extensively between the two world wars and were joined in 1929 by Rice Brothers, who marketed their houses under the slogan 'Rices' Remarkable Resi-dences'. It was during this period that the Cassiobury, Tudor and Kingswood estates were constructed in the private sector and the first ventures in housing by the Urban District & Borough Councils appeared at Sydney and Eastbury Roads, Rose Gardens, Leavesden Green, Willow Lane, Wiggenhall and by far the largest,

the previously mentioned Harebreaks estate. This whole process was accelerated by the extension of the Metropolitan Railway into Buckinghamshire and Hertfordshire and the line was completed as far as Watford in 1925. The Company made great play about the advantages of living in what it was pleased to call 'Metroland' and this produced the tart phrase about 'Building homes for metrognomes.'[17]

It is interesting to trace the architectural influences at work in twentieth century England in general and Watford in particular, especially in the domestic field, and one of the most important was that of Richard Norman Shaw, who besides designing public and commercial buildings, laid out the first planned garden suburb in this country at Bedford Park in 1875. It was then in the open countryside of Middlesex but is now just another part of the metropolitan sprawl near Turnham Green Underground Station. One of his favourite architectural devices was an early seventeenth century type of venetian window still to be seen on contemporary houses and flats being produced by Rice Brothers. Charles Voysey was also an important source of inspiration. The semi-circular bay windows and triangular gables of his house of 1887 at Shackleford in Surrey come through clearly in the work of Charles Brightman in Cassiobury Park Avenue, Kelmscott Crescent and on the Cassiobury estate generally. Also two of Voysey's most important houses, The Orchard,[18] built for himself in 1900-1 and Hollybank of 1903-4, both in Chorleywood would have been well-known locally. The same is also true of Tilehurst in Grange Road, Bushey, of 1903 and Myholme in Merry Hill Road of 1911. Two other architects certainly ought to be mentioned. One is Philip Webb, who built The Red House, Bexley, for William Morris, as this had a marked influence on later generations because of its simple and dignified appearance. The other is Charles Rennie Mackintosh, the designer of the world famous Glasgow School of Art, but more especially in this context for Hill House at Helensburgh. Both contributed detailing that architects and builders all over the country were grateful to exploit.

In addition to individual contributions, the total effect of planned suburbs and towns such as Bedford Park from 1875 onwards, Port Sunlight from 1888 onwards, Bourneville from 1895 onwards, but above all Letchworth, which was begun in 1904 to be followed by Hampstead Garden Suburb started in 1907, were to have a marked influence on the Cassiobury estate, while the passion for the greatness of the age of the first Elizabeth, that produced far more olde oake beames up and down the country than the sixteenth century itself, is represented by the Tudor estate of Rice Brothers.

Outside the sphere of housing the two decades from 1920 to 1940 saw the rise of the cinema and the multiple store and these two influences succeeded in making nearly every High Street in the country look the same. From this period only two buildings really make any impact in Watford. One is the Town Hall, designed in a sober neo-Georgian style by C. Cowles-Voysey, the son of Charles Voysey. It emphasises functionalism and utility rather than the civic ostentation of previous eras, when the world was ransacked for architectural details to embellish buildings, the main object in life of which seemed to be a desire to keep down the unemployment figures rather than the rates, by providing work for an army of cleaners in a host of

nooks and crannies. The other is Odhams Printing Factory, seen best from North-Western Avenue where its impressive scale and mass can be appreciated. The architect was Sir Owen Williams, who was an engineer by training and also designed other outstanding buildings such as the Peckham Health Centre, Lilley and Skinners in the Pentonville Road, Sainsbury's warehouse in Rennie Street, Southwark, all of 1935 and above all Boots factory at Beeston on the outskirts of Nottingham of 1932 and 1938. Odhams is therefore a building of much more than local significance and this seems most appropriate in a town with one of the greatest concentrations of printing in the world. Both the Town Hall and Odhams have roof lanterns that recall Ragar Östberg's Stockholm Town Hall of 1909-23, a building much admired in the twenties and thirties. Before crossing the great divide of the Second World War, reference should be made to the Metropolitan Railway Station of 1925, now owned by London Transport. This could so easily have been too obtrusive, but passes itself off neatly as part of the leafy Cassiobury Park Avenue around it, in a quiet, unostentatious manner which is the essence of matching a building to its surroundings. From today's standpoint, it was a curious place to put a railway terminus and only used as such because plans to push the line as far as the High Street came to nothing. The present G-Plan furniture shop was originally designed to fulfil this role.

The period since the Second World War has been marked by great changes. Schools, such as Chater of 1909 and the Watford Grammar Schools for Girls and Boys of 1907 and 1912 respectively,[19] which followed the pioneering work of E. R. Robson and T. J. Bailey for the London School Board and were designed in a kind of Queen Anne or neo-Dutch style, have given way to the light airy designs of Hertfordshire County Council, as exemplified in Cassiobury, Francis Combe and Langleybury Schools, to pick only three outstanding examples. Both the Holywell and Meriden housing estates, designed by the architectural section of the Borough Engineer's Department, are excellent examples of pleasant buildings allied to good landscaping. The temptation to build a host of tower blocks has been resisted and the only two in the town are on the Meriden estate. This has meant that in grouping and mass, housing has remained on a human scale, unlike many areas in London, which now resemble poor imitations of New York. Office construction has been almost entirely confined to the Clarendon Road area, where large Victorian houses have been demolished to allow for this development. Here, as with similar buildings elsewhere in the country, the influence of the Modern Movement is obvious. Perhaps the most intriguing of the post-war structures are the Shrubbery, Church Street and Sutton Road multi-storey car parks. When seen at night with bands of light alternating with concrete ramps, they seem to float above the ground like shrines to the twentieth-century deity of the internal combustion engine. By day they appear much more utilitarian, but even so the one at Church Street makes an elegant contrast with St. Mary's, the Free School and the Bedford Almshouses.

At the time of writing, the future lies quite literally all about us as the new Central Area Redevelopment Scheme is within sight of completion. In a few short years, this greatest engineering project in the town since the advent of the railway will have been absorbed into the life of Watford and it will be extremely difficult to

visualise what was there before. In the process, the former road pattern will have been altered drastically, and by the use of landscaping and pedestrian precincts an entirely new town centre will have emerged.

On turning to the naming of streets, it is wise from the beginning to have one or two basic principles clearly fixed in the mind. The medieval, manorial, farm and field names often with even older backgrounds are naturally found in the area around the High Street, but also in the parts of the town developed since the First World War, where a conscious effort has been made to recall the past. In addition to names connected with locality, prominent citizens and benefactors are in this way commemorated. The Victorians however lived in an expanding, thrustful age, the momentum of which did not begin to decline until the Edwardian period and they were not interested in the past when it came to the naming of streets, if only because they were too pre-occupied with making history and ruling the Empire.

Although from 1870 onwards street naming in Watford came under the general supervision of the Local Board of Health, it was done mainly by builders and developers and they were not backward in using their own names and those of children or other relatives for this purpose. They also showed what would now be considered an incredible deference to the nobility, gentry and politicans of the day although, in what at that time was a solid conservative town boasting within its near environs at Bucks Hill a public house called the True Blue, it should be recorded in passing that both the Earl of Derby and Lord Salisbury had streets named in their honour because they were Prime Ministers, but Disraeli never achieved this eminence. Perhaps he was considered too clever by half compared with Gladstone, who although a Liberal had his name used for a street, presumably because in 1868 he had the good sense to appoint the locally very popular Earl of Clarendon as his Foreign Secretary. In this connection it should be recalled, that in an age not used to instant news from the television screen, memories of past events and people remained alive for far longer.[20] Also in a world that lacked film and television stars, football heroes or pop music idols, the gap was filled by politicians, whose speeches were reported at inordinate length in the press and were dissected down to the last detail in public houses. It is therefore not surprising that politicians were high on the list of people likely to be considered for street names in Victorian and Edwardian times. Standing above the day to day life of the country was the Throne and a formidable number of streets were named after people who had some connection with Queen Victoria, while the area just north of the railway bridge over the St. Albans Road is a paean of praise occasioned by her Diamond Jubilee.

In general I have made entries for those names with an interesting background, even if on the surface they appear to be rather pedestrian and especially if there is some local link with wider events, but I have omitted those about which there can be no doubt. For example, I have included King and George Streets but excluded King George's Avenue. Many streets have a linked or common history and I have normally grouped these together under one heading and relied on cross references to guide the reader. It should also be mentioned that research has been made much harder by large gaps in early general, special and water rate books and by the fact that most business records of small Victorian builders have long since vanished. In

the body of the text I have generally not cited the actual documents when tracing the development of a name through several centuries, as I feel that this would have impeded the flow of the narrative. I have relied instead on the Bibliography on page 100 to carry the reader on to the sources from which information has been obtained. Finally, I have occasionally strayed outside the present Borough boundary if the street concerned has strong associations with the town, and have left out some streets I would have liked to include, because I can find no reasonable explanation for the name used. However, one of the most satisfying things about any piece of research is that it would be most unfair not to leave some unsolved problems for future workers in the same field, and I am happy to think that I have honoured this obligation.

NOTES ON THE INTRODUCTION

1. For the origin of the name of the town, see the Watford entry in the main sequence of street and place names.
2. The name was changed to the present Grand Union Canal in 1929.
3. I have used Cassiobury Estate for the property owned by the Earls of Essex and Cassiobury estate for the housing development built there after the First World War. I have also used a capital 'E' generally for other private Estates and a small 'e' for the subsequent housing estates that replaced them.
4. Charles Hadfield. British Canals. David & Charles, 1969. This gives an account of the effect of railways on canals, especially in chapters 11 & 12.
5. Evening Echo. June 17th 1970. Page 1.
6. I can trace no documentation which gives a lead about an architect except for one intriguing possibility. The owner of the property in 1822 was Stewart Marjoribanks. From the evidence of a former Watford resident, which came into the hands of the then Borough Librarian, George Bolton, in 1927, Marjoribanks 'started to take down the top storey' late in 1822. Construction work was carried out on the site in 1825, but it is not clear whether this was for an entirely new building or the remodelling of an earlier one. In 1826 Marjoribanks sold Watford Place to Jonathan King and in the 1840's was residing at a house called Bushey Grove, which was built for him by George Basevi, but has since been demolished. If Basevi was commissioned by Marjoribanks in the 1840's might he not also have designed or remodelled Watford Place in the 1820's? The evidence of style is inconclusive and in any event it would have been a very early work. Basevi was one of Sir John Soane's most brilliant pupils and had a distinguished career until he was killed by falling from scaffolding while examining the western bell tower of Ely Cathedral. If Watford Place were therefore his work, it would mean that it is a building of more than local significance.
7. George Thomas Clark, Superintending Inspector to the General Board of Health. Report to the General Board of Health on a Preliminary Inquiry into the Sewerage, Drainage and Supply of Water, and the Sanitary Condition of the Inhabitants of the Town of Watford. Printed by W. Clowes & Sons for Her Majesty's Stationery Office, 1849. Page 4. In addition, see Appendix 5 for earlier descriptions of the town by various topographical writers.

8. This is an example of paying your money and taking your choice. The Illustrated London News of July 30th 1864, gave the architect as John Collier. A week later it changed its mind and quite unblushingly ascribed the building to Thomas Charles Sorby. By date and design it seems more likely to be the work of the latter rather than the former.

9. A long, descriptive and highly laudatory article in the Illustrated London News of September 9th 1871, contains the highly revealing phrase 'No money has been lavished on mere ornament'.

10. George Thomas Clark, Superintending Inspector to the General Board of Health. Report to the General Board of Health . . . 1849. Page 8.

11. Watford Local Board of Health. Reports upon Complaints and Nuisances compiled by Unknown Officials of the Board between 1853 and 1856 (manuscript entries). There were considerable changes in the staff of the Local Board during this period. The first two entries could well have been the work of Thomas Redford, who was dismissed in November 1853, and the latter two of W. R. Cranstone who resigned in November 1856.

12. See Appendices 1a and 1b for a full list of these plaques.

13. D. Elliston Allen. British Tastes. Hutchinson, 1968. This work gives a perceptive account of the sturdy regional differences that still exist in the United Kingdom.

14. The term 'New Town' was used after 1850 to denote the area north of the High Street along the St. Albans Road and near the railway station. The post office at 2, Langley Road still has the words 'New Town T.S.O.' displayed on the outside of the building. The developers of the proposed new estate in 1908 merely took this name and moved it further north. It would also have had the advantage from their point of view of associating the new development in people's minds with the Nascot Wood district rather than working class housing in Callowland.

15. Watford Urban District Council. Municipal Watford and its Housing Scheme. 1920. This contains complete details of the building of the Harebreaks estate.

16. Several sleepers from the original track of the London & Birmingham Railway were built into one wall of the Church.

17. I have not been able to trace the exact origin of this quotation, but assume that it must have come from a disgruntled commuter, who was persuaded to buy a very small house on a very large mortgage.

18. This may well have just been a rather typical English country name, but it seems possible that as one of Voysey's first houses, 14, South Parade, Bedford Park, was only a short distance from the entrance to a road called The Orchard, the choice would also have had a certain sentimental appeal.

19. It is typical of the views about education then prevailing, that although the opening of the Watford Grammar School for Boys in 1912 was reported at great length in the Watford Observer of March 23rd, the same ceremony at the Watford Grammar School for Girls in 1907 was not even mentioned. The Grammar School for Boys was designed by Russell and Cooper of Gray's Inn Square and the reporter in the Watford Observer was obviously so overcome

by the occasion, that he delivered himself of the following homily: 'The design of the building is for economical reasons plain in character, of a simple Georgian style, which has become the recognised traditional manner of architecturally expressing the English grammar school.'

20. R. C. K. Ensor. England 1870-1914. O.U.P., 1936. On page 2 the author recalls a conversation held in 1900 with a Somerset countryman, in which the latter compared the eminence of a local worthy in the neighbourhood with that of Lord Palmerston on the national scene. Palmerston had then been dead thirty-five years.

MAIN SEQUENCE OF STREET AND PLACE NAMES

ACADEMY ROAD see CAMBRIDGE ROAD

ACME ROAD
Acme was the Greek word for the highest point or the point of perfection, but truth rather sadly compels one to record that it was used in this instance at second hand in honour of the Acme Tone Engraving Company, which set up business here when the road was laid out in 1896.

ADDISCOMBE ROAD see HOWARD CLOSE

ALBANS VIEW
This was built on the site of a triangular piece of woodland called Albans Wood and is above the 300' contour with a view of St. Albans to the north-east.

ALBERT ROAD   ALBERT STREET   ALBERT TERRACE
Watford has no Consort Street, but makes up for this deficiency by having two thoroughfares named Albert. The Prince Consort (1819-61) was still in early middle age when killed off by the bad drains at Windsor. A street was built in 1862 next to Queen's Road and its date and position made it natural that it should have been named after the recently deceased Albert. Up to 1871, what is now Albert Road was part of Weymouth Street and had a row of houses in it called Albert Terrace. During that year the Prince of Wales almost succumbed to the same enteric fever that carried off his father, only this time the drainage system responsible was at Sandringham. However, on December 14th, the exact tenth anniversary of Albert's death, the Prince made a sudden recovery. Up to this time the monarchy had been growing steadily more unpopular because of Queen Victoria's gloomy seclusion after her husband's death, but the Prince's illness and subsequent recovery caused a great wave of sympathy to sweep through the country. In the wake of this changed outlook, it would have been wholly natural to rename a part of Weymouth Street, Albert Road, and thus recall an earlier tragic loss made all the more poignant by the recent providential deliverance.

ALDBURY CLOSE see APPENDIX 2

ALEXANDRA ROAD see DENMARK STREET

ALMOND WICK
The name probably came from 'Alms Wick' meaning a piece of enclosed land near the Almshouses. This was close to St. Mary's Church and in 1841 the National Schools building was erected there to provide elementary education. It was used later as offices by the firm of solicitors, Sedgwick, Turner, Sworder and Wilson and then to house the Registrar of Births, Deaths and Marriages. It was finally demolished to make way for the Church Street multi-storey car park.

ARMAND CLOSE
Armand David Blackley (1891-1968) was a well-known local art connoisseur, who for many years was a managing director of the London art dealers, Bourlet & Sons Ltd. He was at one time President of the Watford and Bushey Art Society and also Chairman of the Management Committee of the West Herts Hospital Group,

besides being active in many other organisations and charities. He also donated a very pleasing group of paintings to the Watford Public Libraries. It was therefore most appropriate, that when two short streets were built off Nascot Wood Road and Ridge Lane at the end of the 1960's, they should have been named Armand and Blackley Closes respectively.

ASCOT ROAD

The Ascot summer meeting in June has always been one of the highlights of the racing calendar, as well as providing endless copy for fashion writers. Edward VII was a keen supporter of the turf and one of the Ascot races, the Queen Alexandra Stakes, was named in honour of his wife. She was always a very popular figure in the country and when in 1913 a road was laid out south of the Rickmansworth Road, Ascot was an obvious name for it, especially as in the same year Queen Alexandra instituted the rose day for hospitals, which has been called after her ever since.

ASHBY ROAD

It was naturally common throughout the country to find builders naming streets after themselves in areas which they had helped to develop. In Watford, Edwin Clifford, William Judge, Robert Ashby and the Waterman family were responsible for the names of Clifford and Judge Streets, Ashby Road and Waterman Close.

ASYLUM ROAD see ORPHANAGE ROAD

THE AVENUE

This originally ran from Stratford Road towards the St. Albans Road and a short road called Nascot Avenue on the same line was pushed out towards it from the St. Albans Road. Rather like the Central Pacific and Union Pacific Railways in America, which linked up at Promontory, Utah, on May 10th 1869, the two roads met in the middle, but needless to say there is no record of a golden paving stone being laid to mark the occasion in 1929 when the word 'Nascot' was dropped and the new road became simply 'The Avenue'.

AYNHO STREET see also CLIFTON ROAD and MILTON STREET

William Gough, of the builders Clifford and Gough, was born in the Northamptonshire village of Aynho and when he developed four streets to the north of Vicarage Road between 1890 and 1893, he used names from his boyhood haunts in Northamptonshire and Oxfordshire. This accounts for Aynho, Banbury, Oxford and Souldern Streets and also for a large number of terraces within streets, which often bear names from this same part of the country. As the firm also produced monumental masonry, distinctive plaques were carved to carry these terrace names and a considerable number still survive in parts of the town developed before the First World War. The most outstanding designs for these plaques had a decoration of scrolls and foliage, but several other plainer varieties were also made. For those interested in hunting them down, I have included details of the ones with scrolls and foliage in Appendix 1A and of the plainer types in Appendix 1B. In addition, photographs of them appear on page 60. William Gough's passion for Oxfordshire caused him to name his own home at 185, Harwoods Road, Oxford House and

explains why Edwin Clifford, who provided the initial capital for the firm, lived at Tusmore Lodge in Alexandra Road.

BALLARD'S BUILDINGS

Just off the site of New Street stood a row of late seventeenth century cottages, which were demolished in 1926. For a period prior to 1838 they were called Dyson's Yard or Buildings, but between that date and 1849, the property was acquired by William James Ballard (1799-1867). The actual date of acquisition was probably 1846, as there is a large and imposing tombstone in St. Mary's church-yard to John Dyson, who died on December 7th 1845. The Dyson family were brewers in the town and it was from them that Joseph Benskin purchased the Cannon Brewery in 1867[1]. In the 1851 census, Ballard was described as a farmer of 200 acres at Colney Butts, employing eight labourers and was resident at Watford Field House. He was also a member of the Local Board of Health from 1852 to 1855 and again from 1862 to 1867 and is recorded as having held the office of deacon at Beechen Grove Baptist Church from 1863 to 1867.[2] In addition, he was thought to have been a sub-contractor for the embankment between Bushey and Watford on the London and Birmingham Railway, prior to the opening of the section between Euston and Boxmoor in 1837, and as he was a farmer, the equip-ment for digging and carting would certainly have been available. There is no documentary evidence of anyone named Ballard being involved in railway con-struction work, but as sub-contracting was often a haphazard affair, this is not surprising and does not mean that he did not take part in the project. There has always been a tradition in Watford that some of the navvies working on the line were housed in the cottages and even that they were built specifically for this pur-pose. However, as the investigators of the Royal Commission on Historical Mon-uments in the volume for Hertfordshire state quite clearly that the cottages pre-date the railway by some 150 years, it seems more likely that a few navvies merely found lodging there.[3] This view is strengthened by the anonymous account of the building of the Watford Tunnel in the periodical Household Words, where the temporary shanty town constructed for the navvies is described in some detail.[4] In 1851 when the world was admiring the Crystal Palace, which Joseph Paxton had designed to house the Great Exhibition in Hyde Park, 226 people were crammed into thirty-nine out of the forty-two minute buildings which the census recorded as 'occupied'. Doubtless this figure was low, as at least two of the cottages were euphemistically described as lodging houses. This view is supported by an official of the Local Board of Health when on October 26th 1853, he describes the cottages as having from 300 to 400 occupants.[5] In 1855 a water rate was being levied on various donkeys and horses, that formed the principal business assets of sundry rag-and-bone men, sweeps and general dealers. At the time of their demolition, Ballard's Buildings had become one of the most notorious slums in the town and few can have regretted the passing of such unsavoury premises.

BALMORAL ROAD

When the area north-east of the junction of Gammon's Lane and the St. Albans Road was being developed from 1900 onwards, patriotic fervour was at its height

over the Boer War. It was only three years since the Diamond Jubilee and although Diamond and Jubilee Roads were specific marks of the great event, such was the esteem for Queen Victoria, that it seemed only natural to name five more roads after her royal palaces. These were Balmoral, Buckingham, Osborne, Sandringham and Windsor Roads.

BEDFORD STREET
In 1580 Francis Russell, Earl of Bedford, founded the Bedford Almshouses opposite St. Mary's Church, 'that eight poor women . . . might inhabit and be maintained in the said almshouses'. Before the 1870's Bedford Street was known as Leviathan Road and the change occurred between 1871 and 1876. It was perhaps, however, not the original charitable foundation but the extremely influential Duke of Bedford of that period who was being commemorated, as in 1878 Lord Beaconsfield wrote to Queen Victoria that 'the Duke of Bedford is the wealthiest of your Majesty's subjects; his income absolutely exceeding £300,000 a year!' The present nearby Leviathan public house sports a delightful monster on its signboard, which although anatomically splendid is historically inaccurate, as the Leviathan in question was in fact a famous railway engine.

BEECHEN GROVE
The old line of Beechen Grove ran from the western end of Derby Road past the bottom of Sutton Road, up what is now the southern end of Estcourt Road and along the present Gartlet Road to Clarendon Road. A Baptist Church or Meeting House was built there in 1721 and Meeting Alley gave access to it from the High Street. A new Church was built in 1835 and was replaced by the present one in 1878 with its frontage on Clarendon Road. In the days when it was a pleasant country lane it was presumably shaded by beech trees. The section which is now Gartlet Road was renamed in 1935 and called after Gartlet School, which was situated in a building on Clarendon Road. The present line of Beechen Grove into Clarendon Road and onwards to the new central roundabout was the result of road alterations in 1962 and 1972.

BEECHPARK WAY
The Grove was the residence of the Earls of Clarendon from 1753 until 1935 and at the point where Grove Mill Lane joins the Hempstead Road stood two lodges. The one on the north side was called London Lodge and the one on the south side, Beech Lodge or Great Beech Tree Cottage, and it was on the site of the latter that Beechpark Way was built. As Grove Mill Lane marked the border between the Grove and the Cassiobury Estate, London Lodge was a lodge to the Grove and Great Beech Tree Cottage a lodge to the Cassiobury Estate.

BELGRAVE AVENUE
Watford was fortunate in having large landowners living on its borders, who took a great interest in the development of the town. Lord Belgrave, 1st Marquis of Westminster (1767-1845), owned and developed the area of Westminster which became known as Belgravia and his third son, Robert Grosvenor (1801-1893), was created Lord Ebury in 1857 and lived at Moor Park. He was a noted Liberal M.P., one of the chief opponents of the High Church movement and also closely associ-

ated with the 7th Lord Shaftesbury in promoting factory reform. The Grosvenor family provided numerous M.P.'s for Chester and South Cheshire from the sixteenth century right up to the 1870's and all these family connections gave Watford the names of Belgrave Avenue and Chester, Ebury, Grosvenor and Shaftesbury Roads.

BELLMOUNT WOOD AVENUE
Bellmount Wood was an area of woodland about 300 yards from north to south and 150 yards from east to west that stood on the site of Trefusis and Berceau Walks rather than what is now Bellmount Wood Avenue.

BENSKIN ROAD
Joseph Benskin came to London from Leicestershire at the age of thirteen and after a great deal of hard work, made his way in the hotel business. In 1867 he moved to Watford and bought Dyson's Brewery also known as the Cannon Brewery. The concern grew until his death in 1877 and then other members of the family expanded the undertaking still further until Watford ales became available throughout the south of England. In 1957 Benskin's Watford Brewery was merged with the Ind Coope organisation, now part of Allied Breweries, but the name of the Compasses Inn in the High Street was changed to the Joseph Benskin, to perpetuate the memory of the original firm and its founder.

BERCEAU WALK
One of the meanings of the French word 'berceau' is an arbour or bower and there was a Berceau Walk in the grounds of Cassiobury House. This association with the past was preserved completely intact when a short street on the Cassiobury estate was given the name.

BERRY AVENUE see APPENDIX 3

BERRYGROVE ROUNDABOUT
This well-known junction of the M.1. and the A.41. is a permanent reminder of the departed Berrygrove Wood, whose ghostly glades, once the delight of courting couples, now echo only to the roar of passing exhausts.

BIDDENHAM TURN see APPENDIX 2

BIRCH ROAD
This road existed from 1900 until 1924 as an access road from Wiggenhall Road to the south west corner of Watford Fields. In the middle 1920's it disappeared from the map and Lammas Road was extended across Elfrida Road to the bridge under the railway. At the same time Tucker Street was also shortened to its present length, thus cutting off its access into Wiggenhall Road. William Tucker for many years a Councillor and Alderman of Watford Borough Council, was the owner of the land on which Tucker Street was built and as Birch and Neal were the surnames of closely related parts of his family he was therefore instrumental in naming all three of these streets.

BLACKLEY CLOSE see ARMAND CLOSE

BLACKWELL DRIVE
Part of the Oxhey Estate was sold in 1877 to Thomas Blackwell of the firm of Crosse & Blackwell and his descendants lived at Oxhey Place.

BOARD OF HEALTH ROAD see LOCAL BOARD ROAD

BOVINGDON CRESCENT see APPENDIX 2

BOWMANS GREEN see APPENDIX 2

BRADSHAW ROAD
The land owned by John Buller Bradshaw in the area of the present Bradshaw Road came on the market in 1896 and was an important factor in opening up the whole of the Callowland area for housing development in Victorian and Edwardian times.

BREAKSPEARE CLOSE
The father of Nicholas Breakspear in later life became a monk of St. Albans and it seems extremely likely that Nicholas himself was born on a farm at Bedmond called Breakspeare Farm. He was the only Englishman ever to become Pope and took the title of Adrian IV. Although he was a mild man, his pontificate from 1154 until his death in 1159, was set in very stormy times. In his youth, he would have known Watford well and is commemorated by streets on the Harebreaks estate named Breakspeare Close, Nicholas Close and Pope's Lane.

BRETT PLACE
Dr. Alfred Thomas Brett (1828-1896) received his professional education at Guy's Hospital and was a man of great energy, who in addition to holding many public offices, including that of Medical Officer of Health to the Watford Urban District Council, was a tireless advocate of all kinds of improvements in the area. He was one of the leading lights in the founding of higher education and the public library service, a keen supporter of the provision of houses through building societies and greatly interested in making allotments available for working men. He was for many years a freemason, a member of the Watford Company of the Hertfordshire Volunteers and a director of the local Gas Company. In politics he was a Liberal and the only slight criticism that could be found in a long obituary in the Watford Observer was that he was a strong supporter of funeral reform, 'even going so far as the advocacy of cremation as a sanitary precaution.'

BRIDGER CLOSE see THORPE CRESCENT

BRIDLE PATH see SHADY LANE

BRIGHTON ROAD see REGENT STREET

BRIGHTWELL ROAD see also LONGSPRING
This is a name dating back at least to the twelfth century when the word used was Brithewelle. Variations on this were Brutewelle in 1223 and Brittewelle in 1225. By 1436 the present spelling was being used and probably means simply a bright or clear spring of water welling out of the ground. It is also the name of a farm which

still exists and which in the seventeenth and eighteenth centuries was known as Hatter or Hatter's Farm. The derivation of the latter is obscure, although it could be connected with the name of a farmer tenant or owner. However, the fact that it was also a field name makes it possible that it could have been derived from the Old English 'haehdeor' meaning 'deer' as at Hattersley (deer wood) in Cheshire, especially as both Longspring and Deerspring were areas of woodland, in which deer may well have been raised.

BRIXTON ROAD

This is the only instance outside Brixton itself where the name has been used for a street in the whole Greater London area. It was named by William Judge, the local builder, who had business connections in this part of South London.

THE BROADWAY see QUEEN'S ROAD

BROMET CLOSE

Mary Pownall was born at Bedford Leigh in Lancashire and spent her early youth in Middlewich and Knutsford with time away at school in Newark. She studied art at Frankfurt-on-Main, Paris and Rome and her sculpture was exhibited widely in this country and abroad. In 1902 she married Alfred Bromet, who was a barrister, and came to live at Lime Lodge in Heath Road, where she remained until her death in 1937. Her best known works from the point of view of Watford are the figures on the war memorial originally outside the Peace Memorial Hospital and now on the north-east side of the Town Hall. It is also worth noting that Lime Close, which runs parallel to Heath Road, was named after Lime Lodge. By a curious coincidence, the house in which Mrs. Bromet was born at Bedford Leigh was also called the Limes.

BRUCE GROVE

When this road next to Yarmouth and Cromer Roads was built in 1899, it was first quite logically going to be called Norfolk Road. However, by 1900 business premises called the Bruce Grove Works had appeared and the name was changed to the present one. Norfolk Avenue was built in 1932 by Rice Brothers and was so named because Norwich was their home town.

BUCKINGHAM ROAD see BALMORAL ROAD

BUCKNALLS LANE

Bucknalls is a house that was built in 1855 and now forms part of the Building Research Station. In a tithe map of 1838 Bucknalls Lane appears as Bucklers Lane and it seems probable that the name of the lane was changed when the house was built. This may be the family name of a former owner of the land on which the house was built, but the only local occurrence of Bucknall is as a branch of the Grimston family of Oxhey Place and there is certainly no documentary evidence of land ownership by them in North Watford.

BUCK'S AVENUE

Buck's Lane is shown on the 1871 Ordnance Survey map as a country lane running south-east from Pinner Road and the present Buck's Avenue is only a section of it.

It hardly seems likely that it owes its name to parading Regency dandies or male rabbits or deer. During the seventeenth and eighteenth centuries the Buck family were local landowners of substance. From 1703 to 1728 Sir William Buck and his son Charles were in possession of the Grove, while from 1652 to 1712 Sir John Buck (Sir William's father) and Sir William himself owned the estate called Hillside lying in the three parishes of Ridge, Shenley and Aldenham. There is no documentary evidence to connect the Buck family with this particular area of land in Oxhey, but it seems not unreasonable to keep them in mind when trying to determine the origin of the name.

BUSHEY MILL LANE
This is one of the medieval roads of Watford that meandered out of Bushey past Bushey Hall, Busheymill Bridge and Bushey Lodge Farm to the St. Albans Road. It first appears in directories showing housing development in 1908, but even today its rustic origins are only too apparent to the motorist anxious to speed on his way.

BUTCHER'S ESTATE
The land east of Clarendon Road and north east of the High Street as far as the railway line to Rickmansworth was developed for housing in the 1860's and 1870's. Part of this was owned by Thomas Estcourt (see the entry for Estcourt Road) but two other sections of it were known as the Butcher's and Waterfield Estates. In Kelly's Post Office Directory of Hertfordshire of 1851 there is an entry for John Butcher, a tailor in the High Street. In the 1850's he owned property near Red Lion Yard and also in another unspecified part of the High Street. Much more significantly in this latter area, he also owned what was described as 'a meadow.' It therefore seems likely that Butcher's Estate was situated between the High Street and the land owned by Thomas Estcourt and therefore refers to the area now covered by Queen's and Derby Roads, Albert Street and Carey Place. Also in the 1850's Jonathan King, the owner of Watford Place (see the entry for King Street) owned land in the Water Field district and this was presumably what is now the site of Ebury and Shaftesbury Roads and the Water Fields recreation ground.

BUTTERWICK see APPENDIX 3

THE BY-PASS
North-Western Avenue, which is part of the A.41., runs from the Hempstead Road at its junction with Gipsy Lane in a south-easterly direction back into London and successive lengths in the Borough are known as Gade Side, Colne Way and Otterspool Way with Elton Way falling just outside the boundary. This plethora of names is really of no avail as it has been known to Watfordians for over forty years simply as 'the By-Pass'.

BYRON AVENUE see MILTON STREET

CALLOWLAND
In 1379 the name first appears as Calloweland and means 'bare land'. There was a Callowland Farm situated in what is now Cecil Street and also an area of woodland called Callowland Spring at the junction of the present Ridge Lane with Nascot

Wood Road. As with Longspring, it could well have been an enclosed area for raising game. The whole district was opened up for housing in the 1890's after the Earl of Essex had purchased it in 1881 from its former owners, the Master and Fellows of Merton College, Oxford. An alternative name for the area was Gamell, which was mentioned in a document of 1633, although it was probably used at an earlier date. This latter was most likely to have come from a proper name, as Gamel was an Old Norse word meaning simply 'old' and has come down as the very rare surname Gamell. Somebody of this name may well have been a now long forgotten owner or tenant of Callowland Farm.

CAMBRIDGE ROAD

George, 2nd Duke of Cambridge (1819-1904), was a cousin of Queen Victoria and Commander-in-Chief of the Army from 1856-1895. In 1862 he was made a Field Marshal and from 1870 fought a long rearguard action against the military reforms of Edward, Viscount Cardwell. After the death of the Prince Consort, he carried out many official and social duties and was made A.D.C. to the Queen. In 1897, the year in which this road was laid out, he was awarded the G.C.V.O. From 1898 to 1910, the part of Cambridge Road running into Granville Road was known as Academy Road, presumably because the Duke, who was very interested in training, was also President of the Military Academy at Woolwich during his period of office as Commander-in-Chief. He took these duties seriously and his famous annual inspections became known as 'Duke's Days'. In 1947 the Academy was amalgamated with the Royal Military College to form the Royal Military Academy at Sandhurst. The Duke was also a noted eccentric and on one occasion while attending service at Kew Parish Church, he startled the congregation with the words 'By all means', after one of the clergy said 'Let us pray'. At another time in the same church when prayers were being offered for the alleviation of a long drought, he remarked loudly that although personally he had no real objection to this method of approaching the Almighty, he very much doubted whether it would be effective while the wind remained in the east, an observation as endearing for its theological quaintness, as its sturdy grounding in the agricultural interests common to other Hanoverians such as George III. One significant local event, which would have reinforced the choice of name, was the opening of the London Orphan Asylum by H.R.H. Princess Mary of Cambridge, Duchess of Teck, in 1871.

CANNON ROAD

The Cannon Brewery of Messrs. Benskins, which is now part of the Allied Breweries combine, was in existence by at least 1750, although the connection between heavy ordnance and strong ale has never been established, except the obvious one between customer and supplier. It seems likely that some early practitioner of the art of advertising merely thought that a cannon would be a peppy brand image.

CANTERBURY ROAD

It appears probable that the humble lamb rather than dreaming cathedral towers was responsible for Canterbury Road. Canterbury, Wellington and Westland are

provincial districts of New Zealand and the three roads named after them were being built in the period 1890 to 1892. Large scale refrigeration started in 1882 and by the early 1890's, frozen lamb was flooding onto the English market and making a significant addition to the meat supplies of the late Victorian era. This new trade link and the quickening interest in New Zealand generally would have made the three names selected a natural choice at this time, but I can find no specific local reason for their use in Watford. The southern part of Westland Road had at one time been called Weymouth Street North.

CAPELL ROAD

Cassiobury House and Park came into the hands of the Capel family by the marriage of Elizabeth, great grand-daughter of Sir Richard Morrison with Arthur, Lord Capel, of Much Hadham. Although he was executed during the Civil War and the property sequestrated by Parliament, it was returned to the family at the Restoration. In 1830 the 6th Earl of Essex had Capel changed to Capell and from that date the latter spelling of the name became general. The road was constructed in the late 1850's when Oxhey was being developed and although it obviously honoured the family generally, it would have been surprising if a cause célèbre of half a century previously had not had some bearing upon the matter. The Honourable and Reverend William Robert Capel was Vicar of St. Mary's from 1799 to 1854 and belonged to that great body of eighteenth and nineteenth century clergy, who were more interested in sport than their cure of souls. He was at one time master of the Old Berkeley Hunt and provoked a famous law-suit with his half-brother the 5th Earl of Essex, by taking the hunt over the latter's land at Cassiobury on April 1st 1809, when he had been expressly warned not to do so. Although the Earl of Essex won the case, it proved no more than a temporary setback for hunting generally and certainly did little damage to the reputation of the Honourable and Reverend William Capel. However, the latter always continued to use a single l at the end of his name and the spelling with two l's would have been a useful way of emphasising to people that the Earl of Essex and not the Vicar of St. Mary's was being honoured in this way.

CAPELVERE WALK see DE VERE WALK

CARACTACUS GREEN

Although Caractacus may have been an ancient British chieftain, there was also more importantly for Watford a racehorse of the same name, which won the Derby in 1862. The noble animal was owned by Charles Snewing of Holywell Farm, who was also a prosperous publican in the Tottenham Court Road.[6] This notable success was made the occasion for a vast celebration given to local labourers and workhouse inmates, at which 800 lbs of roast beef, quantities of plum pudding and 1400 quarts of ale and porter were consumed. A large marquee was erected and there was a great profusion of flags and bunting. The fife and drum band of the Watford Rifle Volunteers played music in the grounds and in the evening a ball was given by Snewing for his friends. Caractacus was a complete outsider at 40 to 1 and Snewing had made £20,000 on the race, so even a celebration of this magnitude

could hardly have dented his resources more than a fraction. Before the race Bell's Life had published the following verse:

And if, of the outsiders there,
Just one should pass the winning chair,
Enrolled in the successful three
Be sure Caractacus is he.

The writer may have been an execrable poet, but he was certainly an excellent tipster.

CARDIFF ROAD

In the 1880's, 1890's and early 1900's, Cardiff was one of the premier ports of the country with coal from the South Wales mines being exported all over the world. At this time it was second only to London in the volume of its exports and third only to London and Liverpool in the volume of its imports.[7] During the two decades after 1861 Cardiff Castle had been rebuilt by William Burges for the 3rd Marquis of Bute in a style of medieval fantasy that would have made any self-respecting Briton of the Middle Ages stop dead in his tracks. It was in 1893 at this high point in the history of the port, that Cardiff Road was laid out in Watford.

CAREY PLACE

Jonathan Carey was a plasterer, who came to work on the old Beechen Grove Baptist Chapel built in 1835, which was the predecessor of the present building of 1878, and later helped to develop property in the area of the street which bears his name. For many years the only whitesmith's shop in South-West Hertfordshire was situated here.

CARISBROOKE AVENUE

The Marchioness of Carisbrooke opened a new club house at the Grims Dyke Golf Club in Oxhey Lane, Harrow, in October 1936 at the time this road was being constructed. The event was widely reported in the local press at the time and Carisbrooke Avenue now provides a permanent reminder of it.

CASSIOBURY

The earliest known form of the word is Caegesho in 793 meaning Caeg's spur of land (hoh) and seems to be identical in origin with Keysoe in Bedfordshire. The suffix 'bury' almost certainly comes from the medieval word 'burh' denoting a manor, and Cassiobury not Watford was mentioned in Domesday Book. Many variant spellings, the most important being Cashio, are used in documents and have given rise to a number of interpretations of its meaning. The most ingenious is that it derives from Cassivelaunus, an ancient British chieftain, information about whom is in inverse proportion to the number of Romans he is supposed to have turned into mincemeat with the scythes on his chariot wheels. Cassiobury House and Park were from the time of the Restoration until 1922 the property of the Earls of Essex and on the development of the property and other land in the neighbourhood for housing, the name was used for Cassio Road, Cassiobridge Road, Cassiobury Drive and Cassiobury Park Avenue.

CASSIO HAMLET see HEMPSTEAD ROAD and THE HIGH STREET

CAXTON WAY see GREENHILL CRESCENT

CECIL STREET

Cecil is the family name of the Earls of Salisbury and Hatfield House in Hertford-shire is their family home. When the area to the north of Watford Junction was being developed in the late 1890's and early 1900's, it was during the famous 3rd Earl's third period of office as Prime Minister from 1896 to 1902 and he thus was the inspiration for Hatfield Road and Salisbury Road. He was not however the inspiration for Cecil Street, as the latter was named after Cecil Judge, the son of William Judge, who built the nearby Judge Street.

CHALK HILL

The Ordnance Survey map of 1871 shows a chalk pit at the junction of Pinner Road and Aldenham Road and the Bushey Lime Works opposite the Watford Gas Works on the other side of the London and North Western Railway. Thus the name not only marked an outcropping of the chalk but also the fact that it had been worked and formed the basis for a thriving industrial concern. The site of the Bushey Lime Works is now occupied by the Colne Valley Water Works.

CHARLOTTE'S VALE see HYDE ROAD

CHERRYDALE

The junction of Hagden Lane and Rickmansworth Road was called Cherrydell Hill Corner and at this point stood the 'Hagney' Lane Turnpike gate when Rickmans-worth Road was part of the Reading and Hatfield Turnpike Trust (1770-1881). In the same area fronting Rickmansworth Road was also a house called Cherrydell, while on Hagden Lane opposite the entrance to Mildred Avenue, was another house called Cherrydale. When it was demolished and new housing developed in 1968, the road thus created, retained the old name. From this weight of evidence, it seems obvious that not just a few isolated trees, but whole cherry orchards must have existed here at one time. This view is supported by Chauncy, the County historian, who wrote in 1700, 'In the south-western angle of the county, near Rickmansworth and Watford, are many orchards, the apples and cherries from which find a ready market in London'. It was also in this area that one of the last known polecats in Hertfordshire had its home.

CHESTER ROAD see BELGRAVE AVENUE

CHILCOTT ROAD see FULLER GARDENS and FULLER ROAD

CLARENDON ROAD

This road was cut through from the High Street to the Junction Station in 1864 for the dual purpose of giving a quick access to the railway and providing space for new housing. It is natural that it should have borne the name of the Earl of Clarendon, as one of the principal local landowners, and it had many large houses standing in their own grounds. These have been demolished steadily since the Second World War to make way for large-scale office development. At the junction of Clarendon Road and the High Street, the western corner is known as Clarendon Corner and the eastern as Dudley's Corner after a former firm of costumiers.

CLARKE WAY see THORPE CRESCENT

CLIFFORD STREET see ASHBY ROAD

CLIFTON ROAD see also AYNHO STREET and MILTON STREET
Clifton and Westbury-upon-Trym are both suburbs of Bristol and when two roads were built out of St. James' Road parallel to Cardiff Road in 1875, it would have been completely logical to name them after districts within this other great port, which faces the chief city of Wales across the Severn Estuary. However, both Clifton in North Oxfordshire and Westbury in North Buckinghamshire are villages only a few miles from Aynho, the birthplace of William Gough of the building firm of Clifford & Gough, and it therefore must be assumed that he was responsible for naming them. This assumption is strengthened by the fact that both roads are just on the other side of Vicarage Road from Aynho, Banbury, Oxford and Souldern Streets, which William Gough developed and also named in memory of the places he would have known intimately in his youth.

CLIVE WAY see COLONIAL WAY

CLYSTON ROAD
The Watford Parish Registers date from 1539 and the first marriage recorded in them was between John Clyston and Elizabeth Kyne. It seems almost certain that if John Clyston himself could have known that a road was named after him in twentieth century Watford, he would have been more than a little startled at this totally unexpected rise from rural obscurity to urban fame.

COATES WAY see THORPE CRESCENT

COBB GREEN
Under the terms of the will of John Falcon, the manor of Garston was sold to Henry Cobb and on his death in 1873 it passed to his widow, Mrs. Mary Anne Cobb, who retained it until the end of the nineteenth century.

CODICOTE DRIVE see APPENDIX 2

COLE KINGS
This was a farm on the south side of Hagden Lane where the present road turns a sharp right angle just south of Belgrave Avenue. A variation of 1728 was Cold Kings and the meaning is obscure. In Essex 'Cole' appears as a corruption of 'Colne' for the river that reaches the sea through the estuary below Colchester, and in Watford this may in fact simply be a piece of ground once owned by a man called King which is situated near the River Colne. Alternatively it may have referred to ownership by the Monarch, as the Crown held the Manor of Watford from the Dissolution of the Monasteries until 1609. A building, that appears to have been the former farmhouse, still remains.

COLE ROAD
James Cole, a contractor and well known local figure, lived in Local Board Road during the 1860's and was at one time owner of land at Colney Butts.

COLNE AVENUE   COLNE WAY
The first reference in a Hertfordshire document is to Colenea in 785 with the 'ea' suffix meaning a stream or river, but here and in other parts of the country where the name occurs, the origin is obscure.

COLNEY BUTTS
The word 'butt' was often used to describe a small piece of land that abutted or bordered onto a larger holding and was also the term for a practice range, especially in connection with archery. There is no evidence however of archery ever being practised here, and although colney is sometimes used as a corruption of coney meaning a rabbit, the nearness of the river makes it more likely that this was simply a small area of ground close to the Colne, rather than scrubland infested by rabbits or men with long-bows. The farm buildings of the property were roughly at the present junction of Vicarage and Occupation Roads and at the time of the 1851 census were in the possession of William Ballard, the owner of Ballard's Buildings.

COLONIAL WAY
> Far called, our navies melt away;
> On dune and headland sinks the fire;
> Lo, all our pomp of yesterday
> Is one with Nineveh and Tyre.[8]

Those still in early middle age can remember Empire Days, when schools were paraded en masse in playgrounds to sing patriotic songs about the Empire on which the sun never set. Vast quantities of Union Jacks were always available on such occasions and it was considered very superior to have one with the King's head in the middle. It is now somewhat ironical to look back and see that Colonial, Federal, Imperial, Rhodes and Clive Ways were named in the 1940's, 1950's and early 1960's when the Commonwealth as a down-to-earth, voluntary association of states had replaced British delusions of imperial grandeur. Perhaps the most perceptive comment on the whole subject is the following jingle:

> What I like about Clive
> Is that he is no longer alive
> There is a great deal to be said
> For being dead.[9]

COMBE ROAD see also FULLER GARDENS and FULLER ROAD
Francis Combe and Elizabeth Fuller were the founders of public education in Watford. Over sixty years before Elizabeth Fuller's Free School was started in 1704, Francis Combe, by a will of 1641 left 'ten pounds for ever, to a free school in Watford, in the County of Hertford, for teaching the poor there to cast accounts, to read English, and to write.' It is therefore wholly appropriate that this pioneer of education should be commemorated by the Francis Combe County Secondary School in Horseshoe Lane.

COMET CLOSE
It is perhaps now difficult to recall the horror aroused in 1954 when two De Havilland Comets disappeared out of the blue skies, one near Elba and the other

close to Stromboli, but it was the intensive work done on metal fatigue after these crashes that has played an extremely important part in modern air safety. It was in recognition of this and also to mark the long association of the De Havilland Company with the Borough, that two short streets on the edge of Leavesden Aerodrome were named Comet Close and Trident Road after the firm's famous aircraft.

COMYNE ROAD see FULLER GARDENS and FULLER ROAD

CONINGESBY DRIVE

Coningsby was the name of the maternal grandmother of the 5th Earl of Essex (1757-1839) who included it in his surname when he succeeded to her property. He was a well-known patron of the arts and Whig politician and at different times was M.P. for Westminster, Lostwithiel, Okehampton and Radnor. When the road was named, an extra 'e' was slipped into the middle when nobody was looking.

COW LANE see also APPENDIX 3

This was formerly a quiet lane leading from Lea Farm to Otterspool, which took its name from a nearby field called Cow Pasture. Until the end of 1970 it ran from the St. Albans Road nearly to the M.1., but from the beginning of 1971 the section to the east of the Watford to St. Albans railway line was renamed York Way as a memorial to the work done by Councillor 'Bert' York for the town generally, but especially for his own constituents in the Knutsford Ward and also as a mark of his service for the Meriden Community Association.

COWPER CLOSE

Mary Cowper took a keen interest in the life of St. Mary's Church and in 1632 granted by deed to trustees, certain estates in Warwickshire, so that the resultant income should be given to the Vicar of Watford and his successors to encourage them 'to take pains in the preaching of the Word of God in the Church and Parish.' She also left money for the poor of both Watford and Kings Langley.

COX'S CORNER

The junction of Hartspring Lane and North Western Avenue is known as Cox's Corner after the firm which makes car seats and office furniture. The firm has now moved to the Midlands, but the name is likely to be used for many years yet.

CRANFIELD DRIVE see APPENDIX 3

CRONJE ROAD see ROBERTS ROAD

CROOK LOG

The south side of the stretch of London Road from Haydon Road to Merry Hill Road, which now has Bushey Manor County Primary School, the Bushey Day Nursery, the County Council Yard and other business premises, used to be known as Crook Log and the use of the name lingered on until very recently. In the nineteenth century there was a small brickfield and a row of cottages with a public house called the Merry Month of May, which existed until the outbreak of the Second World War. In the eighteenth century it had been a desolate length of road

frequented by footpads, who from time to time attacked travellers entering Watford, and it was even rumoured that the notorious Dick Turpin had operated here, although like Robin Hood and Jack the Ripper, his reputation ensured that his name was linked up and down the country with incidents, about which there existed no credible evidence. An earlier version of Crook Log in 1626 was Croked legg, but its meaning seems totally obscure, unless the unsavoury reputation of the area at that time signified that the name was an intelligent anticipation of the American slang for gangster. Support for this totally untenable theory is given by the fact that in 1425 a version of the nearby Merry Hill appears as Meryhell. It should also be recorded that 61, Chalk Hill, was called Crook Log House and from 1882 until the early part of the First World War was occupied by Joseph Clemson Benskin, Chairman of the Watford Urban District Council from 1898 to 1899 and one of the sons of Joseph Benskin, the founder of Benskin's Brewery. After this it became a girls' School and was only finally demolished in the early 1960's to make way for the present Dorchester Court.

CROSS MEAD see APPENDIX 3

CROSS STREET see ESTCOURT ROAD

CUFFLEY AVENUE see APPENDIX 2

DEACON'S HILL
At first glance, it would appear that there must be some ecclesiastical reason for the name, but in fact the Deacon family were for generations the owners of Wiggen Hall and as the oldest son was always called Thomas, a footpath in the grounds became known as Tommy Deacon's Hill. It seems a pity that the 'Tommy' was dropped from the name when the nearby lane was reconstructed in 1927, to become the present Deacon's Hill.

THE DEATH TRAP
The junction of Queen's Place and Radlett Road with the two bridges under the railway by Ebury Road are known collectively in the area as the Death Trap. This nick-name commemorates a pedal cyclist, who was killed on the acute bend when his machine went out of control.

DELL ROAD   DELL SIDE
In 1307 there was mention of a Robert Ate Delle and there was also a Dell Wood in the general area where these two roads are situated. It is also worth noting that there was reference to a 'Dellfeild' in 1618.

DELLFIELD CLOSE see APPENDIX 4

DENMARK STREET
Denmark Street runs parallel to Alexandra Road and into Malden Road and thus produces the intriguing possibility of its having been named for two separate and almost equally valid reasons. Firstly, Arthur Capel, who was created Viscount Malden and Earl of Essex, was in 1670, appointed Ambassador to the Court of Denmark and secondly, Princess Alexandra was a Danish princess. She was married

to the Prince of Wales in 1863 and these streets were laid out at the end of the 1860's. Such was the great rejoicing in Watford at the royal marriage, that in spite of Essex Road running parallel to Malden Road, Arthur Capel's seventeenth century Ambassadorship to the Court of Denmark must yield gracefully and gallantly to the more contemporary claims of Princess Alexandra's wedding. Development in this area took place slowly and even on the 1871 Ordnance Survey map no houses were shown as having been built in Alexandra, Essex or Malden Roads or Denmark Street.

DERBY ROAD see ESTCOURT ROAD

DEVEREUX DRIVE
Robert Devereux, 2nd Earl of Essex (1566-1601), was at one time the great favourite of Queen Elizabeth, but fell from grace and was executed for high treason. His son, also called Robert, 3rd Earl of Essex (1591-1646), had his title restored by James I and led an upright but hardly distinguished political career and became a parliamentary general in the Civil War. Because the Capel family had supported Charles I, their Estates at Cassiobury were granted to Robert Devereux in 1645. He died without issue the following year and at the Restoration, the Estates reverted to the Capel family, who were created Earls of Essex to replace the extinct Devereux lineage.

DE VERE WALK see also CAPELL ROAD
De Vere is one of the family names of the Earls of Essex. It is a surname of great nobility and antiquity and was held by a long line of the Earls of Oxford. On the death of the 20th Earl of Oxford in 1703 De Vere became extinct in the Oxford family, but passed by a daughter, Diana, to the 1st Duke of St. Albans, whom she had married in 1694. In 1825, Lady Caroline Janetta Beauclerk, 3rd daughter of William, 8th Duke of St. Albans, became the first of the three wives of Arthur Algernon Capel, 6th Earl of Essex, and De Vere has been combined with Capel (after 1830, Capell) as part of the family name of the Earls of Essex ever since.

DIAMOND ROAD
Sale plans for parts of the Callowland area were drawn up in 1896 and both Diamond and Jubilee Roads appear on them and were a patriotic anticipation by the developers of Queen Victoria's Diamond Jubilee in 1897. What nobody could have foreseen was that this highly popular choice would be reinforced by the Prince of Wales' horse 'Diamond Jubilee' winning the Derby in 1900.

DOME ROUNDABOUT
The Dome roundabout stands at the junction of North-Western Avenue and the St. Albans Road and is so named not because it is dome-shaped, but after the nearby Dome garage. This became one of the Blue Star chain of garages in 1960, but by then the name had been so firmly established that it is never likely to be changed.

DUDLEY'S CORNER see CLARENDON ROAD

35

DUKE STREET

Duke and Earl Streets appear on the 1871 Ordnance Survey map, and it seems clear that they gratified, in a rather general way, the Victorians' passion for touching their caps metaphorically to the nobility. However, Prince Street, which does not appear on the 1871 Ordnance Survey map, but was built soon afterwards, followed closely on the serious illness of the Prince of Wales at the end of 1871 (see the entry for Albert Road) and this event probably gave strong impetus to the choice, which also completed a neat sequence of noble precedence from south to north, starting with Earl and continuing through Duke up to Prince.

DURBAN ROAD

Many British towns have streets named after places, battles or commanders prominent in the wars of the nineteenth century. The Crimean, Afghan, Ashanti, Zulu and South African campaigns all produced their quota, and when two streets were being built in Watford at the height of the Boer War, it was natural to name one after Durban, the principal town of the very English Natal and the other after Pretoria in the Transvaal, where Lord Roberts liberated 3000 British prisoners of war when he captured it in June 1900.

EARL STREET see DUKE STREET

EASTBURY ROAD see HAMPERMILL LANE

EASTLEA AVENUE see APPENDIX 2

EBURY ROAD see BELGRAVE AVENUE

ESSEX LANE see HUNTER'S LANE

ESSEX ROAD see MALDEN ROAD and DENMARK STREET

ESTCOURT ROAD

Thomas Henry Sutton Sotheron Estcourt (1801-1876) was the son of Thomas Grimston Bucknall Estcourt of Estcourt near Tetbury in Gloucestershire. Thomas Grimston was a minor politician, who was content to sit as M.P. for Oxford University from 1827 to 1847, where he persistently opposed every parliamentary and religious reform. Thomas Henry was educated at Harrow and Oriel College, Oxford. In 1829 he entered parliament and until 1865 represented in turn Marlborough, Devizes and North Wiltshire. He married a wealthy heiress called Lucy Sarah Sotheron in 1830 and in 1839 took his wife's name in lieu of his own on succeeding to Darrington Hall, Yorkshire, the property of the Sotheron family. However, he resumed the paternal name of Estcourt in 1855, two years after his father's death. He was forced to retire from public life in 1863 because of a paralytic seizure, but lived on until 1876. For the brief period of four months during 1859 he was Foreign Secretary in the second ministry of the 14th Earl of Derby, of whom he was a great friend and admirer. During the late 1860's, land which Thomas Henry owned between Clarendon Road and the railway was developed for housing and his convenient abundance of names gave the town Sutton, Sotheron and Estcourt Roads. In addition, his political connections were responsible for Derby and Lower Derby

Roads, also constructed in the late 1860's and for Stanley Road in the 1870's, clearly named after Lord Stanley, who became the 15th Earl of Derby on the death of his father. He was a considerable politician in his own right and held the office of Foreign Secretary from 1874 to 1878 in Disraeli's second cabinet. Finally, there is very good reason to suppose that Cross Street built in 1868 was named after Richard Assheton Cross, who was a protégé of the 14th Earl of Derby and a contemporary of the 15th Earl of Derby at Rugby and Trinity College, Cambridge, as it was also in 1868 that Gladstone was defeated sensationally by Cross at an election in South-West Lancashire. After this success, the latter went on to a distinguished Parliamentary career, which lasted until the end of the century.

EUSTON AVENUE
Euston Square in London was named in 1825 after Lord Euston, the son of the Duke of Grafton. The first section of the London and Birmingham Railway was opened from Euston to Boxmoor in 1837 and in view of Watford's close connection with the development of the line, it is strange that no street was named after the Terminus until 1911. At that time it was possibly felt to be especially appropriate, as the 75th anniversary of the opening of the service was due in 1912.

EVANS AVENUE see THORPE CRESCENT

EXCHANGE ROAD
At first sight this road might seem to have been the commercial heart of Watford from time immemorial with vast quantities of money changing hands day by day. However, the more prosaic fact is that a new telephone exchange was built in 1956 and when a road was cut across Market Street to Upton Road in the late 1950's, it was considered a convenient name to use.

FAIRCROSS HOUSE see APPENDIX 4

FAIRFOLDS see APPENDIX 3

FARMERS CLOSE see APPENDIX 3

FARM FIELD see APPENDIX 3

FARRALINE ROAD see WIGGENHALL ROAD and APPENDIX 4

FARTHING LANE
This was Ferthynglane in 1427 and Farthynglane in 1436 and as it was a very narrow street off the High Street, its name was doubtless used as a term of contempt for its insignificance. It now forms part of the present Watford Field Road and is one of the links between Watford Fields and the High Street.

FEARNLEY STREET see HOWARD CLOSE

FEATHER BED LANE see SHADY LANE

FEDERAL WAY see COLONIAL WAY

FELDEN CLOSE see APPENDIX 2

FIFTH AVENUE see APPENDIX 3

FIRST AVENUE see APPENDIX 3

FOREST ROAD see SHERWOODS ESTATE

FOURTH AVENUE see APPENDIX 3

FRANCIS ROAD see PERCY ROAD

FULLER GARDENS   FULLER ROAD
Mrs. Elizabeth Fuller was the only daughter of John Comyne otherwise called Chilcott of Tiverton in Devon and one of her immediate ancestors had founded the famous Blundell's School. She was a woman of strong personality and at one time owned Watford Place. It was in the grounds of this house that she caused a free school to be built in 1704. This was suitably endowed and remained as a school until 1882. The original building still stands opposite St. Mary's Church and is now used for parochial purposes. Elizabeth Fuller was thus one of the principal founders of public education in the town and her memory is kept very much alive by the fact that all former pupils of the Watford Grammar School for Boys are proud to be known as 'Old Fullerians.'

GADDESDEN CRESCENT see APPENDIX 2

GADE AVENUE   GADE SIDE
The name of the river Gade seems to be a back formation from Gaddesden, which itself was a combination of the Anglo-Scandinavian feminine personal name Gunnhild and 'ea' meaning stream. The name is first mentioned in 1242 as 'Gatesee'.

GAMELL see CALLOWLAND

GAMMON'S LANE
Gammon's Farm was situated slightly to the east of the junction of the present Comyne Road and Gammon's Lane. When the latter was a simple country lane, it wound its way back to the St. Albans Road at a point slightly to the north of what is now Ridge Street and the present road follows the twists and turns of its predecessor. The name probably came from an owner or tenant of the Farm, as the French word 'jambe' meaning 'leg' had a Norman diminutive of affection 'gamb' meaning 'little leg', which gave the surname Gammon.

GANDERS ASH see APPENDIX 3

GARSMOUTH WAY see APPENDIX 3

GARSTON CRESCENT   GARSTON DRIVE   GARSTON LANE
In addition to being the name used for three streets and a park, Garston is employed generally for the surrounding area, which developed from a very small hamlet centred on All Saints' Church. It comes from the Old English 'gaerstun', a grassy enclosure or paddock and was one of the original medieval manors of Watford.

GARTLET ROAD see BEECHEN GROVE

GEORGE STREET see KING STREET

GLADSTONE ROAD
It might be thought that in the middle 1870's a town like Watford with a highly conservative tradition, which even boasted a public house in its near environs at Bucks Hill called the True Blue, was highly unlikely to name a road after Gladstone. However, from 1868 until his death in 1870, the locally very popular 4th Earl of Clarendon was Foreign Minister in Gladstone's first cabinet and thus the Liberal leader was ironically accorded an honour denied to his Conservative rival Disraeli.

THE GLEBE see APPENDIX 3

GOODRICH CLOSE see THORPE CRESCENT

GORLE CLOSE see THORPE CRESCENT and also KELMSCOTT CLOSE

GOSSAMERS see APPENDIX 3

GRANTCHESTER COURT see APPENDIX 4

GREENCROFT CRESCENT
Greencroft Crescent, Warren Avenue and The Mount were to have been three roads just to the south of the present Gade Side. Greencroft Crescent was to have run in a semi-circle from Minerva Drive to Fairview Drive, Warren Avenue would have been built north of Minerva Drive and parallel with it, while The Mount was to have gone north in a straight line from Fairview Drive past the end of Minerva Drive to link up with Warren Avenue. This development was to have taken place in the late 1930's, but the outbreak of the Second World War put paid to the project and it was not revived when peace returned.

GREENHILL CRESCENT
David Greenhill (1876-1947) was one of the most exceptional men ever to be a citizen of Watford. He was born a Londoner, although of mixed Scottish and Sussex descent, and from a printing apprenticeship in Camden Town rose to become Director of the Sun Engraving Company and Managing Director of Sun Printers Limited. He was a technical innovator of outstanding merit with an international reputation, which he enhanced by world-wide travel. In addition he took a keen interest in the town and his most important achievement in this sphere was the support he gave to the Peace Memorial Hospital. In spite of the vital part played by his firm in the Second World War, it is likely that his reputation will rest ultimately on the work he did between the two world wars in the production of periodicals in general and Picture Post in particular. In retrospect it is now quite clear that the latter was a bridge between the Victorian approach of the Illustrated London News and the techniques employed by the cinema newsreel and contemporary television news coverage. It is also no accident and a just tribute to a truly remarkable man, that one of the streets running off Greenhill Crescent was called Caxton Way, after the first English printer.

GROSVENOR ROAD see BELGRAVE AVENUE

THE GROVE

From 1753 until 1925, the Grove was the home of the Earls of Clarendon, who played such a prominent part in the life and history of Watford, although the building itself is just outside the Borough boundary. The name of the house probably derived from one of the original landowners, John Atte Grove, who was mentioned in 1353. In 1939 important documents and part of the staff of the L.M.S. Railway were transferred from Euston to the Grove and British Rail still use it as a study centre for management techniques.

GROVE CIRCUS

This group of houses stood on what was then Beechen Grove opposite the southern end of Estcourt and Sotheron Roads. It was considered better than Ballard's Buildings by only a whisker and finally demolished under a slum clearance order in 1934.

GROVER ROAD

The Grover family owned the land on which this road was built in the 1880's and at that date they were wine-merchants in the High Street.

HAGDEN LANE

It has been suggested that this might be 'hedge dene', a sunken way with hedges on both sides or more ingeniously that the 'hag' part of the name refers to a witch. A much more likely explanation is that the word is a combination of the Old English 'haca,' a bend and 'dell', a valley, as the line of the modern road still follows faithfully the several bends of the former lane.

HAINES WAY see SHERWOODS ESTATE

HALSEY PLACE

Sir Frederick Halsey (1839-1927) of Gaddesden Place was a Conservative M.P. continuously from 1874 to 1906, when he was ousted by the great Liberal landslide. From 1874 to 1885 he was one of the three members for Hertfordshire and after the Reform Act of that latter year sat until 1906 for the Western or Watford division of the County. Besides being Chairman of the Hertfordshire County Council for fifteen years he held many other public offices and was a noted freemason. He also laid the foundation stone for the Halsey Masonic Hall in the Rickmansworth Road in 1925 and dedicated the building in the following year.

HAMILTON STREET

When dealing with streets named Hamilton, it is wise to tread very warily indeed. If a military association is suspected, especially if other streets nearby are connected with the Boer War, then the person involved is almost certainly Sir Ian Hamilton (1853-1947), who served with great distinction in South Africa. He later came within an ace of success during the Dardanelles campaign but at the crucial moment lacked men and ammunition and was recalled to Britain in October 1915. If, on the contrary, a naval connection is thought likely, Lady Emma Hamilton's name springs at once to mind, but the Victorians, while perfectly willing to commemorate a glorious victory of yesteryear by calling streets after Lord Nelson,

were totally disinclined to perpetuate the memory of his extra-marital amatory pursuits by according Lady Hamilton the same honour. In these circumstances it is not difficult to find a much more likely claimant in Lord George Hamilton (1845-1927), who was First Lord of the Admiralty from 1886 to 1892 in the 3rd Earl of Salisbury's second administration. In Watford the position is complicated by Roberts Road, named after Field Marshal Lord Roberts of Boer War fame, being close to Hamilton Road. However, the latter was laid out from 1891 onwards, more than a decade before Roberts Road, and the dating thus coincides with Lord George Hamilton's tenure of office. The importance of his six years' work of reform is now scarcely remembered, but he bids fair to be called the founding father of the modern British Navy. It is not realised today how much H.M.S. Pinafore, which first appeared in 1878, was based on fact rather than fiction. Up to the Crimean War, the wooden walls of England reigned supreme, but after that time new inventions such as armour, turrets, mines and torpedoes were all developed abroad, and even when ironclads were built in this country, such was the Navy's innate conservatism, that they were fully rigged with three masts and had a high poop and forecastle. The not unnatural result of this crass stupidity was that in September 1870 the *Captain* foundered with nearly all hands during a gale in the Bay of Biscay. Between the Crimean War and 1886, naval ordnance was subordinated to the Army, which retained a passion for muzzle loaders. Such depths of incompetence were plumbed, that at a famous gunnery trial held at Portland in 1872, the Navy's crack gunner missed his target from two hundred yards range. Anybody who could bring order to chaos of this all-encompassing magnitude and clear out Augean stables of such immense proportions, was an obvious choice for a street name, especially as in spite of all its sins of omission and commission, the Service still roused great patriotic feeling in the hearts of most Britons.

HAMPDEN WAY see APPENDIX 4

HAMPER MILL LANE
A mill at Oxhey is mentioned in the Domesday Survey and about 1300 was called Hanpole mill. In 1374 this was Hanpole mulle and by 1556 had become Hamper myll and appears to be derived from the Old English word 'hana', a cock, thus meaning 'cock-pool.' At the Dissolution of the Monasteries it became the property of George Zowche and was known popularly as 'Souches Mill'. Until the middle of the eighteenth century, it had been a grain mill, but at that time it was acquired by William Lepard, who conducted experiments with paper-making. In spite of a fire in 1793, paper continued to be made there until 1872, when Joseph Smith, the eccentric owner of that date, locked the building one day and simply left it. Among the bales of paper remaining were large quantities of old Post Office telegram forms with their stamps still attached. These had been sold by the Post Office to a contractor on the understanding that they would be pulped within six months, but he had merely passed them on to Joseph Smith. Except for a certain amount of chewing by rats they then remained undisturbed until workmen were repairing the roof in 1910. Some of these workmen started to sell the stamps on the open market and nobody would have discovered the theft, if some of them had not proved to be

41

forgeries and attracted the attention of dealers. After the First World War the Mill was converted to the delightful private residence now there today. Hamper Mill Lane used to extend as far as the junction of the High Street and Chalk Hill, but the section between Thorpe Crescent and the High Street was renamed Eastbury Road between 1871 and 1890 after the medieval manor of Eastbury, which was situated in this area.

HAREBREAKS

There was a Hare Farm on the site of the present Linden Lea and there is also The Hare public house on Leavesden High Road. It would be tempting to suggest that the area of woodland called 'The Harebreaks', after which the road and the housing estate were named, came from a combination of the words 'hare' and 'break' or 'brake'. This would be woodland from which hares broke out when being chased, or the thickets and groves, which they frequented, although it should be pointed out that the animal normally favours open ground. However, near Berkhamsted, Haresfoot comes from a personal name Hugh Harefot, mentioned about 1200 and Hare Street occurs near Ardeley on the Roman Stane Street and comes from the Old English 'here-straet' and means army street or way. It is therefore possible that the name does not derive from the animal, but a proper name or even has a military connection.

HARFORD DRIVE

The 7th Earl of Essex (1857-1916) married twice. His first wife was Eleanor Harford, who died in 1885 and her name was commemorated by a street on the Cassiobury estate when it was built fifty years after her death in 1935.

HARROD FARM see HARWOODS ROAD

HARVEST END see APPENDIX 3

HARWOODS ROAD

In 1314 mention was made of a John Hereward and Harwoods itself was first recorded in 1506 as a small manor owned by the Monastery of St. Albans. By 1609, it had become incorporated in the Manor of Watford and in the eighteenth century the variant Harrod Farm was in use. After passing through several hands, the property was bought in 1770 by the 4th Earl of Essex and in 1900 the 7th Earl of Essex sold the Harwoods Farm Estate to Charles Brightman, the well-known builder and contractor, who with his partner Robert Ashby, was instrumental in forwarding the rapid growth of Watford during the Edwardian period and after the First World War. As Harry Camp was also at one time connected with this activity, the combination of business interests became known as the A.B.C. Syndicate.

HATFIELD ROAD see CECIL STREET

HATTER FARM see BRIGHTWELL ROAD

HAYDON ROAD see APPENDIX 4

HEALEY ROAD

Charles Healey (1856-1939) was a well-known personality in Watford and for many years was Manager of the Healey Brewery, which was owned by his mother. The enterprise was taken over by Benskins in 1898 and Charles Healey remained a director of the latter until his death. He was a notable soldier, served in the Boer War and was a member of the National Defence Corps in the First World War. He was also an artist of no mean achievement and several of his sketches of old Watford are on view in the Central Library. It was as an after-dinner speaker that he made one of his strongest marks and in a celebrated exchange with the Honourable A. Holland-Hibbert (afterwards Lord Knutsford) he more than held his own. The former was a naval man and an ardent temperance advocate. At a dinner to welcome home those who had fought in the Boer War, he made oblique reference to the Reserve Forces and intoxicating liquor. Charles Healey in his reply said that it was a great mistake for the former speaker to have forsaken salt water for fresh, a sally which brought down the house. In the early 1900's there was a move on the part of the Public Libraries Committee, of which he was a member, to black out betting news in the daily papers and he was scathing in his denunciation of what he considered a manifest absurdity. It is not without a certain irony, which he would have been the first to appreciate after making such a stand, that the road which commemorates him should be next to Caractacus Green, named in honour of the Derby Winner of 1862.

HEMINGFORD WAY

Dennis Henry Herbert (1869-1947) was created 1st Baron Hemingford of Watford in 1943 and served as M.P. for the Watford Division of Hertfordshire from 1918 to 1943. He was educated at the King's School, Ely, and Wadham College, Oxford, and on leaving University qualified as a solicitor and was President of the Law Society in 1941/42. During his long parliamentary career he was the Chairman or a member of several select and departmental committees, and was Chairman of Ways and Means and Deputy Speaker from 1931 to 1943. Despite all his other commitments he found time to be a member of the Hertfordshire County Council from 1912 until his death and was made an alderman in 1933.

HEMMING WAY see THORPE CRESCENT

HEMPSTEAD ROAD

On leaving the centre of Watford, the Hempstead Road passes between the Town Hall and the Central Library to what used to be known as Cassio Hamlet. Besides being the road to Hemel Hempstead, it was also a branch of the Roman Watling Street and part of the Sparrows Herne (Bushey) to Aylesbury Turnpike in the eighteenth and nineteenth centuries. The section between the Town Hall and the Central Library is now a pedestrian precinct.

HERBERT STREET

This was constructed in 1888 and 1889 and was named after Herbert Clifford, the son of Edwin Clifford of the building firm, Clifford and Gough.

HERGA COURT see APPENDIX 4

HERONSLEA see APPENDIX 3

HIBBERT AVENUE see MERIDEN WAY

THE HIGH STREET

Until the middle of the nineteenth century, the High Street and Watford were more or less synonymous. The whole life of this small Hertfordshire town was centred on the High Street and the alleys and courts that led from it. Even in the second half of the nineteenth century, it was still known as Town Hamlet in distinction to Cassio Hamlet, the small group of cottages, which nestled on the edge of Cassiobury House and Park. The courts and alleys had picturesque names taken from public houses, owners of businesses situated there or the trades carried on in them. Up to 1850 the ones called after owners of businesses often changed names as properties were bought and sold. After 1850 however, the Local Board of Health gave many of these alleys and courts numbers, a process which although logical to the official mind, hardly made them more salubrious. Many more written records were naturally made by the Local Board of Health and names current about 1850 tended to become permanent. A good example was Dyson's Yard, which changed ownership, probably in 1846 following the death of John Dyson, and was acquired by William Ballard. From that date the property was known as Ballard's Buildings and retained that name until its demolition under a slum clearance order in 1926. A sprawling market, that dated from the reign of Henry I (1100-1135), was held twice weekly in the High Street on Tuesdays and Saturdays and the lowing of cattle, the squealing of pigs and the bleating of sheep mixed happily with the commerce of shops and numerous market stalls and itinerant traders doing their day to day business. A market hall stood in the middle of the road and survived until destroyed by fire in 1853. Market Street itself was a much later addition and was not cut through until 1888 and is therefore a good example of the Watford habit of naming streets after institutions, which exist elsewhere, as it merely led to the market, but never gave it accommodation. In 1928 the market was finally moved to its present site off Red Lion Yard.

HILL FARM AVENUE   HILL FARM CLOSE

Hill Farm was situated at what is now the north east corner of Leavesden Aerodrome at approximately the junction of Langley Lane with Old Forge Close and Hill Farm Avenue.

HILLRISE AVENUE

In 1908 W. B. Maxwell wrote a novel entitled Hill Rise about the trials and tribulations of a speculative builder called Richard Crunden, who went under the nickname of 'Hedgehog' for his ability to dig himself in against all opposition. Hill Rise was the exclusive part of the town of Medford and when the owner of the whole area died, Crunden bought it at auction, because he was incensed by the Hillrise Tennis Club blackballing his daughter's application for membership. There is a great deal of interesting detail about speculative building and the social customs of

the day, while in the end everything comes right for the goodies. The baddies are hastily swept away under the carpet well before the last chapter, so that there is nothing to mar the final stereophonic sound of wedding bells.

HOLLAND GARDENS see MERIDEN WAY

HOLYWELL ROAD

Holywell Road runs from Harwoods Road to Harwoods Recreation Ground and further to the south-west are Holywell Farm, Holywell Hospital and the Corporation's Holywell Industrial and Housing estates. The name first occurs in a Vestry Book of 1698, but there is no evidence of a well having been discovered in the area. However, the clear, refreshing water of springs or wells, which often flowed when all else had dried up, caused them to be associated with minor deities in pagan times and later on in the Christian era with the Virgin. Thus the name is common throughout the country and although the actual evidence of a well is missing, it seems the most likely reason for its having been used in Watford, especially as it was so close to the similarly designated Brightwell Farm.

HOME FARM DRIVE

This road was to have been built on the Cassiobury estate in the 1930's and was named after the former Cassiobury Home Farm of the Earls of Essex. However, like several other similar building projects in the town of that date, it came to nothing and the name has not been revived.

THE HORNETS

'The Hornets' is the nickname of the Watford Football Club and when, owing to development, a link road was cut between Fearnley Street and Merton Road, it was given this name to honour the team's fiftieth anniversary. The Club responded nobly by gaining promotion to the Second Division of the Football League during the 1968/69 season.

HOWARD CLOSE

Mary Morrison in 1629 appointed trustees to oversee the income from land in Watford and place poor children as apprentices. The trust was renewed by deed in 1824 and two of the principal gentlemen of the town, James Howard and Edmund Fearnley, were named among the trustees of that date. James Howard was also mentioned in 1819 as having subscribed £6. 5s towards 'sinking a well and putting down an engine for public use.' Up to 1903 the present Addiscombe Road was part of Fearnley Street and I can find no reasonable explanation for the change of name.

HUDSON CLOSE see THORPE CRESCENT

HUMBERT'S CORNER

The present Central Library was built in 1928 on part of the site of a large house called Little Nascot. This latter was occupied until 1919 by Humbert & Flint, the well-known and still-existing firm of land and estate agents, who acted in this professional capacity for the Earls of Essex. Up to the Second World War it served as a public health and infant welfare clinic and was not demolished until 1959. It

was thus natural that the junction of the Hempstead and St. Albans Roads should have been known as Humbert's Corner and in former, more agricultural days, it was also the site of one of the principal pounds of Watford.

HUNTER'S LANE

This lane ran originally from Hunton Bridge to Leavesden High Road, but when Leavesden Aerodrome was built, it suffered the indignity of being cut in half and there is now one short section in Hunton Bridge and another in Watford. There was also a private house called Hunter's Hall at what is now the junction of Hunter's Lane and Hill Farm Avenue. To avoid confusion the Hunton Bridge section has been renamed Essex Lane.

HYDE ROAD

Both Hyde and Villiers Roads commemorate the complicated relationship by marriage of the Earls of Essex and the Earls of Clarendon. Charlotte was the daughter of William, the 3rd Earl of Essex (1697-1743), by his first wife Jane and the latter was the daughter of Henry Hyde, Earl of Clarendon. In 1752 Charlotte herself married Thomas Villiers (1709-1786), who afterwards also became Earl of Clarendon, but of a later and different creation. The memory of the link between the two families who held adjacent properties, is also charmingly preserved by a small piece of land on the boundary of the two Estates. This is still called Charlotte's Vale and is situated two hundred yards south of Grove Mill House between the River Gade and the Grand Union Canal.

IMPERIAL WAY see COLONIAL WAY

IVINGHOE CLOSE see APPENDIX 2

JACOTT'S HILL

This is an eminence on the West Hertfordshire Golf Course to the east of Whippendell Woods and seems to originate from a William Jaket, whose name is mentioned in 1450. There is also reference to Jackettes medes in 1505 and Sir Charles Morrison bought Jacketts Farm from Thomas Baldwin in 1620.

JAPANESE TERRACE

This group of houses in Estcourt Road has a Clifford and Gough plaque dated 1868, the year in which the firm was founded. It was also the year which in Japan saw the restoration of the monarchy, the end of feudalism and the beginning of the modern industrial state we know today. These changes in a distant country must have made a considerable impact on William Gough at the time he was starting out in business, as he normally had a predilection for sturdy English names.

JORDANS CLOSE see APPENDIX 2

JUBILEE ROAD see DIAMOND ROAD

JUDGE STREET see ASHBY ROAD

KELMSCOTT CLOSE   KELMSCOTT CRESCENT

William Morris acquired Kelmscott Manor in 1871 and it remained in his pos-

session until his death in 1896. Here he spent some of his happiest times in this flat and watery part of Oxfordshire with its wide vistas of sky, which he loved so much. The Manor itself is now owned by the Society of Antiquaries, which has restored it lovingly and carefully. Frederick Hunt Gorle (1872-1931) was Chairman of the Watford Urban District Council from 1919 to 1920 and such a great admirer of Morris, that he called his own house at the junction of Stratford and Hempstead Roads, Kelmscott, when it was built in 1908. He was also the moving spirit in naming these two streets when they were constructed after the First World War and they are a permanent local reminder of one of the most remarkable artists and writers of Victorian England. Perhaps the last word should remain with the haunting poem which Morris composed and had embroidered on the tester of the great four-poster bed at the Manor:

The wind's on the Wold
And the night is a-cold,
And the Thames runs chill
Twixt mead and hill,
But kind and dear
Is the old house here,
And my heart is warm
Midst winter's harm.
Rest, then and rest,
And think of the best
Twixt summer and spring
When all birds sing
In the town of the tree,
And ye lie in me

And scarce dare move
Lest earth and its love
Should fade away
Ere the full of day.
I am old and have seen
Many things that have been,
Both grief and peace,
And wane and increase.
No tale I tell
Of ill or well,
But this I say,
Night treadeth on day,
And for worst and best
Right good is rest.

KELSHALL see APPENDIX 2

KENSINGTON AVENUE see also BELGRAVE AVENUE
This may have been inspired simply by Kensington being a particularly pleasant London suburb, or, as Belgrave Avenue and Chester Road are close at hand, by the fact that Lord Ebury was a son of the 1st Marquis of Westminster. The latter owned a great deal of Westminster itself and this includes within its boundaries most of Kensington Gardens, the Royal Albert Hall and the Albert Memorial.

KILDONAN CLOSE see APPENDIX 4

KIMPTON PLACE see APPENDIX 2

KINGSFIELD ROAD   KINGSFIELD COURT see APPENDIX 3

KING STREET
Jonathan King was the owner of Watford Place from 1826 until 1851 when he sold it so that part of the grounds could be used for building. A prospectus for development was drawn up by George Alexander Smith, an auctioneer, dated Monday, September 15th 1851. This said that there would be 'Leading out of the High Street an intended new line of Road to Rickmansworth by Colney Butts and the Union,

(now part of Shrodells Hospital) forming valuable Business Stations.' The accompanying map showed King, George and Smith Streets, the first having been up to that date the carriage drive to Watford Place. It was not until the middle of the 1850's that building took place to any extent and the original intention of pushing the road towards Rickmansworth never materialised. The Lodge that stood at the junction of King Street and the High Street was converted to a public house and as a kind of pun was called the King's Arms. Queen's Road was not started until 1860 and so it is clear that King Street, the King's Arms, George and Smith Streets had no royal connection, but sprang from a piece of Victorian land development.

KINGSWOOD ROAD

There was a house called Kingswood to the south of Sheepcot Lane approximately at the point where the North Orbital Road now runs. In addition to being used as a street name, it was chosen for the whole housing estate in that area when it was built in the 1930's.

KNUTSFORD AVENUE see MERIDEN WAY

KYTES DRIVE

This is a derivation from a proper name, as a Geoffrey Kete is recorded in 1294, while a field called Kites Bottom appears in 1798 on Land End Farm. An early Victorian redbrick house called Kytes is still in existence and is used by a Joint Committee of the Order of St. John and the Red Cross to accommodate disabled ex-servicemen.

LADY CAPEL'S WHARF

William Capel, 3rd Earl of Essex (1697-1743) married twice and his second wife was Lady Elizabeth Russell. By her he had two sons and four daughters and although two of these daughters died in infancy, the other two, Lady Diana (1729-1800) and Lady Anne Capel (1730-1804), lived into their seventies, but never married. Both died at Russells, one of the dower houses of the Cassiobury Estate. The property of Russells or Russell Farm was crossed by the Grand Junction Canal when it was constructed during the 1790's and it would have been natural to name the landing place built on the property Lady Capel's Wharf after Lady Diana, the elder of these two maiden ladies. A small signboard on the Hempstead Road giving its position is still visible to any passing motorist not exceeding the speed limit.

LADY'S CLOSE

The house called Lady's Close has been incorporated into the buildings of the Watford Grammar School for Girls, but the name is of a very much earlier origin and presumably comes from a field or piece of land, the income from which helped to maintain an altar to the Virgin Mary in pre-Reformation times.

LAMMAS ROAD see also BIRCH ROAD

Lammas lands were a relic of the medieval open-field system. They were enclosed, but after a crop had been grown, those who had common rights could pasture their animals on them. Fields were opened by the throwing down of fences and this

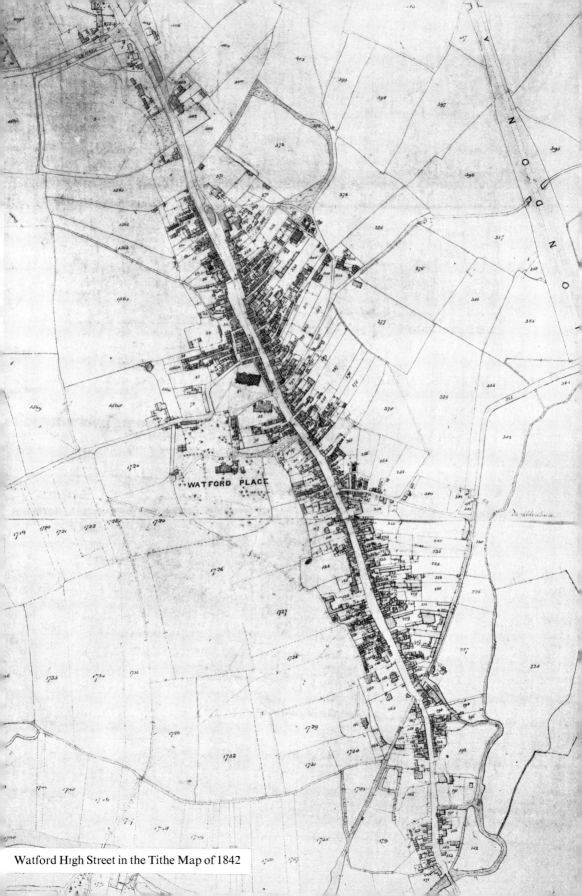

Watford High Street in the Tithe Map of 1842

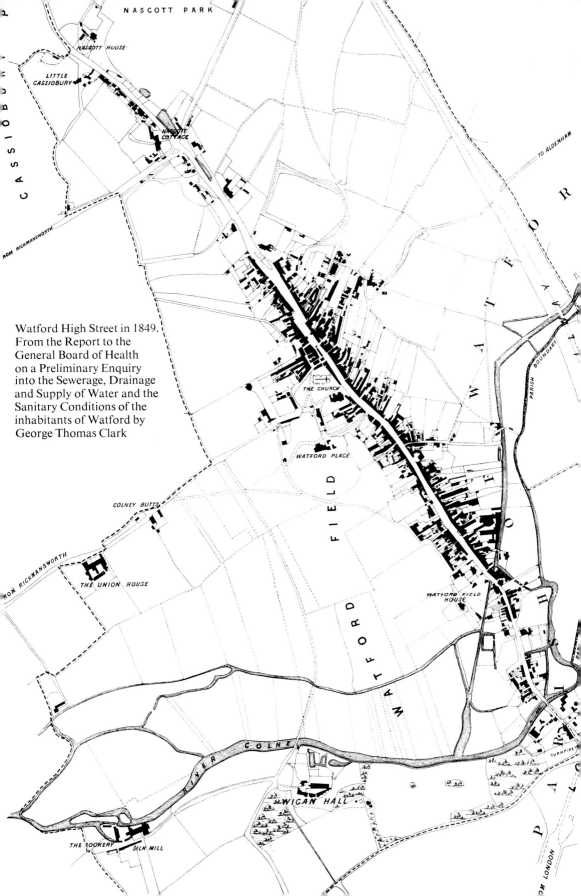

Watford High Street in 1849.
From the Report to the
General Board of Health
on a Preliminary Enquiry
into the Sewerage, Drainage
and Supply of Water and the
Sanitary Conditions of the
inhabitants of Watford by
George Thomas Clark

Watford High Street in the 1871 Ordnance Survey Map

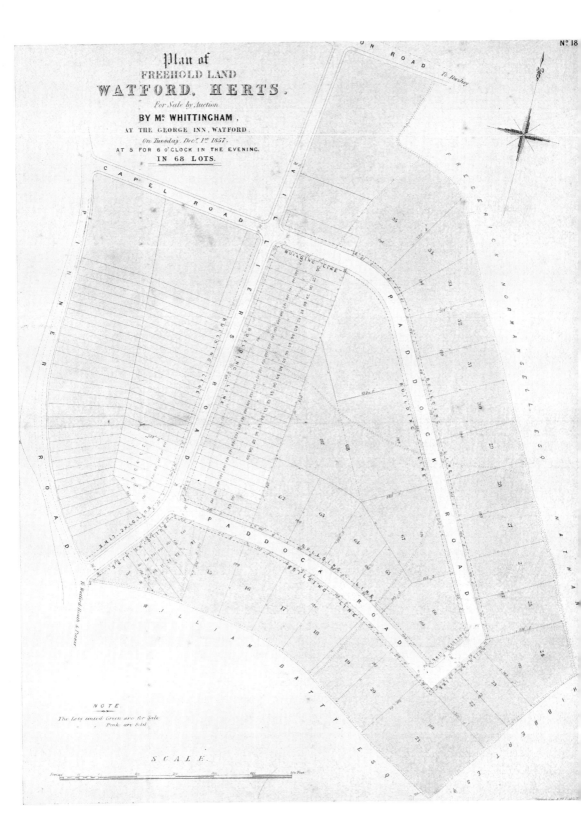

A map showing the development of Oxhey in the 1850s

A map showing the projected New Town development of 1908

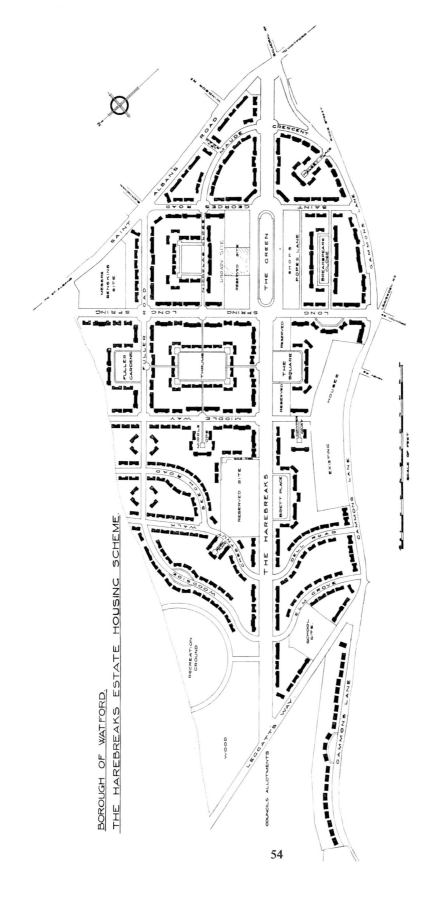

BOROUGH OF WATFORD.
THE HAREBREAKS ESTATE HOUSING SCHEME.

Above:
the layout of the Harebreaks estate. A map based on the one
in Municipal Watford and its Housing Scheme, published by the
Watford Urban District Council in 1920

Below and following three pages:
a contemporary map of Watford with street index

Index to the map of Watford produced for the official Borough Guide 1972

This map is on pages 56 and 57 and the rest of the index follows on page 58

A

Abbey View,	
Garsmouth Way	.. G5
Acme Road ..	.. E6
Acorn Place ..	.. E6
Addiscombe Road	.. E9
Albans View ..	.. E3
Albert Road North	.. E8
Albert Road South	.. E8
Albert Street ..	.. F9
Aldbury Close	.. G5
Aldenham Road	G10-H7
Alexandra Road	E7, E8
All Saints Crescent	.. F3
Appletree Walk	E4, F4
Armand Close ..	.. D6
Ascot Road ..	C9, C10
Ashby Road ..	.. E6
Ashfields ..	D4, D5
Ashtree Road ..	.. E5
Avenue, The ..	.. E8
Avon Close ..	.. F4
Aynho Street ..	.. E9

B

Balmoral Road	E6-F7
Banbury Street	.. E9
Bay Tree Walk	.. D6
Bedford Street	.. E7
Beechen Grove	E8, F8
Beech Park Way	.. C6
Beech Road ..	.. E6
Beechwood Rise	E5, E6
Belgrave Avenue	.. D9
Bellamy Close	.. D7
Bellmount Wood	
Avenue ..	.. C7
Benskin Road ..	.. D9
Berceau Walk ..	C7, D7
Berry Avenue ..	.. E5
Biddenham Turn	F5, F4
Birchmead ..	D7, D6
Birchtree Walk	.. D6
Blackley Close	.. D6
Blackthorn Close	.. E3
Blackwell Drive	E10, F10
Blenheim Close	.. F11
Bovingdon Crescent	.. G4
Bowmans Green	.. G5
Bradshaw Road	E7-F6
Bramble Close	.. E4
Breakspeare Close	.. E6
Brett Place ..	.. E6
Briar Road ..	.. E4
Bridger Close ..	.. G3
Bridle Path ..	.. E7
Bridge Place ..	.. F10
Brighton Road	.. E6
Brightwell Road	D9, E9
Brixton Road ..	.. E7
Broadway, Queen's	
Road ..	.. F8
Bromet Close ..	.. D6
Broom Grove ..	.. D6
Brow, The ..	.. E3
Bruce Grove ..	.. E7
Buckingham Road	E6, F6

Bucknalls Lane	F3-G3
Bucks Avenue ..	.. G11
Burton Avenue	.. D9
Bushey Mill	
Crescent	E6, F5
Bushey Mill Lane	E6-H8
Butterwick ..	.. G5
Byron Avenue ..	.. F7

C

Cambridge Road	E9, F9
Cannon Road ..	.. F10
Canterbury Road	.. E8
Capell Road ..	.. G10
Capel Vere Walk	.. C7
Caractacus Green	.. D10
Cardiff Road ..	E10, E9
Carey Place ..	.. F9
Carisbrook Avenue	.. F7
Caroline Place	.. G10
Cart Path ..	F3, F4
Cassiobridge Road	.. C9
Cassiobury Court	.. C7
Cassiobury Drive	C6-D8
Cassiobury Park	
Avenue ..	C8, D8
Cassio Road ..	E8, E9
Caxton Way ..	.. C10
Cecil Street ..	.. E6
Cedar Road ..	.. F10
Chaffinch Lane	D10, D11
Chalk Hill ..	F10, G10
Chapel Close ..	.. D4
Charlock Way ..	.. D10
Chase, The ..	.. C9
Chequers Lane	.. F1
Cherrydale ..	.. D9
Cherry Tree Road	.. E5
Chesham Way ..	.. C10
Chester Road ..	.. E9
Chichester Way	.. G4
Chestnut Walk	E6, E5
Chilcot Road ..	.. D5
Church Road ..	D7, E7
Church Street ..	.. E9
Clarendon Corner	.. E8
Clarendon Road	.. E8
Clarke Way ..	D5-E5
Clifford Street	.. F9
Clifton Road ..	.. E9
Clive Way ..	.. F7
Clyston Road ..	.. D10
Coates Way ..	F3-G4
Cobb Green ..	.. E3
Codicote Drive	.. G4
Cole Road ..	.. E7
College Road ..	.. E2
Colne Avenue ..	.. E10
Colne Way ..	F5-G6
Colonial Way ..	.. F7
Combe Road ..	.. D10
Comet Close ..	.. D4
Comyne Road ..	.. D5
Conningesby Drive	.. C7
Coppice, The ..	.. E10
Copsewood Road	.. E7
Courtlands Drive	C6-D5
Cow Lane ..	.. F5

Cowper Close ..	.. E6
Cranfield Drive	.. G3
Crescent, The ..	E9, F9
Cromer Road ..	E6, F6
Cross Mead ..	.. E10
Cross Road ..	.. G10
Cross Street ..	.. F8
Crown Passage	.. F9
Crown Rise ..	.. F4
Croxley View ..	C10, D10
Cuffley Avenue	F4, G4

D

Deacons Hill ..	E10, F10
Dellfield Close	.. D7
Dell Road ..	.. E6
Dellside ..	.. E6
Denewood Close	.. D6
Denmark Street	E8, E7
Derby Road ..	.. F9
Desmond Road	.. D5
Devereau Drive	C6, D7
De Vere Walk ..	.. C7
Devon Road ..	.. F7
Diamond Road	.. E6
Douglas Avenue	.. G6
Drive, The ..	.. C5
Dudleys Corner	.. E8
Duke Street ..	.. F8
Durban Road East	.. E9
Durban Road	
West	D9, E9

E

Earl Street ..	.. F8
Eastbury Road ..	.. F10
East Drive ..	.. E5
Eastfield Avenue	.. F7
Eastlea Avenue	.. G6
Ebury Road ..	.. F8
Elfrida Road ..	E9-F10
Elizabeth Court	.. D7
Ellwood Gardens	.. E4
Elm Avenue ..	.. G11
Elm Grove ..	.. D6
Essex Road ..	.. E8
Estcourt Road ..	.. E8
Euston Avenue	.. D9
Evans Avenue	D4, D5
Exchange Road	.. E9

F

Fairfolds ..	.. G5
Fairview Drive	.. C5
Falcon Way ..	.. G4
Falconer Road	.. H10
Farmers Close ..	.. E3
Farm Field ..	.. C6
Farraday Close	.. C10
Farraline Road	.. E9
Fearnley Street	.. E9
Federal Way ..	.. F7
Felden Close ..	.. F4
Fern Way ..	.. E4
Field Road ..	.. G10
Fifth Avenue ..	.. F5
Firbank Drive ..	.. G10

First Avenue ..	F4, F5
Florence Close	.. E4
Forest Road ..	.. E4
Fourth Avenue	F4, G4
Francis Road ..	.. E9
Franklin Road ..	.. E8
Fuller Gardens	.. E6
Fuller Road ..	E5, E6

G

Gade Avenue ..	C9, C8
Gade Side ..	.. C5
Gaddesden Crescent	.. G4
Gadswell Close ..	.. G5
Gammons Lane	D5, E6
Ganders Ash ..	.. E3
Garden Close ..	.. D8
Gardens, The ..	D8, D7
Garfield Street	.. E7
Garnett Close ..	F6, F5
Garsmouth Way	.. G5
Garston Crescent	.. F4
Garston Drive ..	.. F4
Garston Lane ..	F4, G4
Garston Park Parade	.. F4
Gartlet Road ..	.. E8
George Street ..	.. E9
Gladstone Road	F8, F9
Glebe, The ..	.. F3
Glen Way ..	.. C6
Goodrich Close	.. D5
Goodwood Avenue	C5, D5
Goodwood Parade	.. D5
Gorle Close ..	.. E4
Gossamers, The	G4, G5
Grandfield Avenue	.. D7
Granville Road	.. F9
Greenbank Road	.. C5
Greenhill Crescent	.. C10
Green Lane ..	.. F11
Greenwood Drive	.. E4
Greycaine Road	.. F6
Grosvenor Road	F8, F9
Grove Mill Lane	B6, C6
Grover Road ..	.. F10
Gwent Close ..	.. F4

H

Hagden Lane ..	D9, D10
Haines Way ..	D4, E4
Halsey Place ..	.. E6
Hamilton Street	.. F10
Hampden Way ..	.. C5
Harebreaks, The	.. E6
Hare Crescent ..	.. E3
Harford Drive ..	C6, D7
Harris Road ..	D4, E4
Harvest End ..	.. F5
Harwoods Road	D9, E9
Hatfield Road ..	.. E7
Hawthorn Close	.. D6
Haydon Road ..	.. G10
Hazel Tree Road	.. E5
Healey Road ..	.. D10
Heath Road ..	G10, G11
Hemingford Way	.. C5
Hemming Way	D4-E5

55

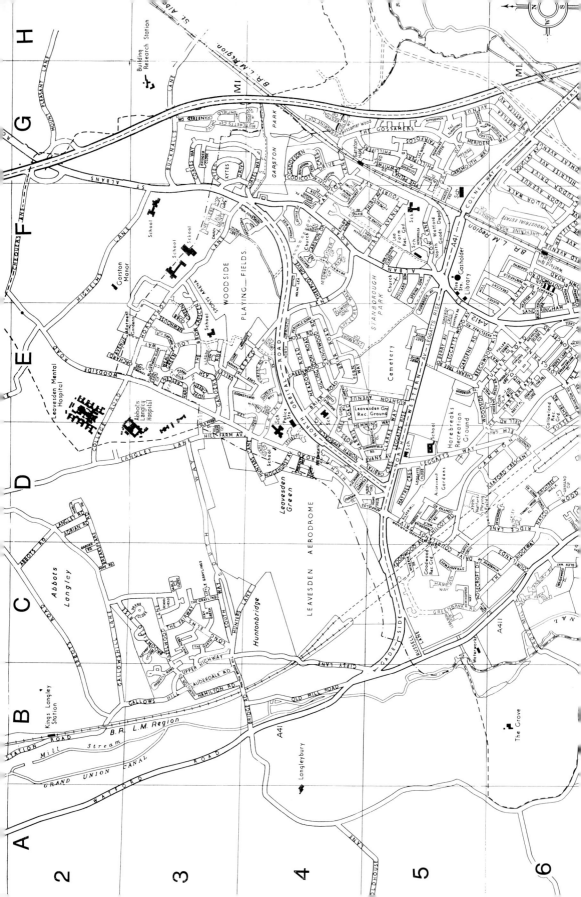

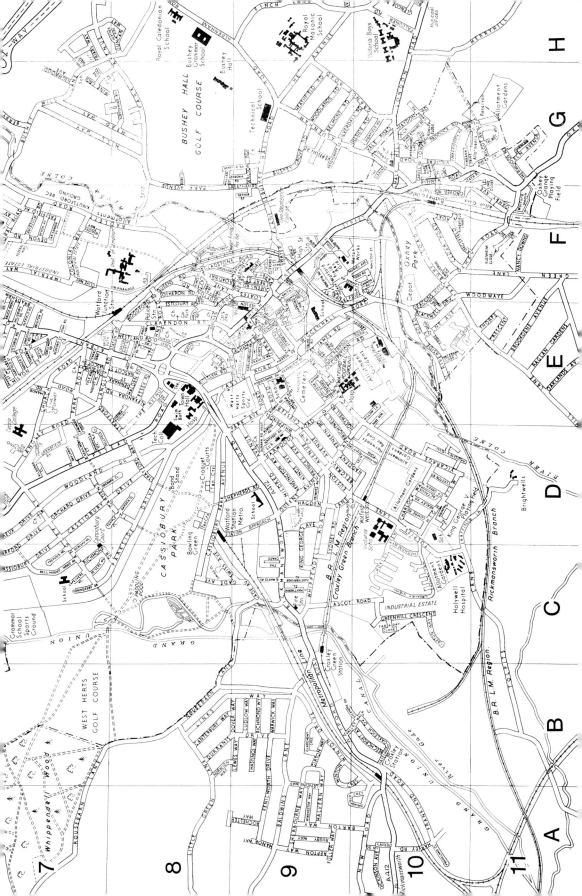

Hempstead Road D7-E8
Herbert Street F9
Herga Court E8
Heronslea F5
Hibbert Avenue F6, F7
High Elms Lane E2, F3
High Road D4-E2
High Street E8-F10
High View D10
Hill Farm Avenue D3
Hill Farm Close D3
Hillingdon Road E4
Hillrise Avenue G6
Hillside Crescent G10
Holland Gardens F5
Holme Lea F4
Holtsmere Close F5
Holywell Road D9, E9
Hope Green E3
Hornets, The E9
Horshoe Lane E3, F3
Howard Close D6
Hudson Close D5
Hunters Lane D4
Hyde Road E8

I

Imperial Way F7
Ivinghoe Close G5

J

Jordan Close D4
Jubilee Road E6
Judge Street E6
Juniper Grove D6

K

Kelmscott Close D10
Kelmscott Crescent D10, D9
Kelshall G5
Kenford Close E3
Kenilworth Court D7
Kensington Avenue D9
Kestral Close G4
Kildonan Close D7
Kilby Close F4
Kimpton Place G4
King Edward Road G10
King George's Avenue C9, D9
Kings Avenue D9
Kingsfield Court F10
Kingsfield Road F10
King Street E9, F9
Kingswood Road E4
Knutsford Avenue F6
Kytes Drive G3

L

Lady's Close E9
Lamb Yard F9
Lammas Road F9, F10
Langley Road D7, E7
Langley Way C7, D7
Langwood Gardens D7, E7
Lansdowne Avenue F4
Larches, The G10
Lavinia Avenue F4
Lea Bushes G5
Leaford Crescent D6
Leander Gardens G6
Leavesden Road E6, E7
Lebanon Close C5
Leggatts Close D5
Leggatts Rise D5-F5
Leggatts Way D5, D6
Leggatts Wood Avenue E5
Lemonfield Drive G3
Leveret Close D4
Lime Close G11
Linden Lea D4-E3
Link Road F8
Liverpool Road E9, E10
Loates Lane F9, F8
Local Board Road F9
Long Barn Close E3
Longcroft E10
Longspring E6
Louvain Way E3
Lower Paddock Road G10
Lowestoft Road E7
Lowson Grove G11
Lych Gate F3

M

MacDonnell Gardens D4
Malden Road E8
Mallard Way G6, G5
Manderville Close D6
Manor Road E7
Market Street E9
Marlborough Road E9
Maude Crescent E6
Maxwell Rise G10
Maythorne Close C9
Maytree Crescent D5
Meadow Road E4
Medway Close F4
Melrose Place D6, D7
Meriden Way G5, G6
Merton Road E9
Middle Ope E6
Middle Way E6
Mildred Avenue D9
Milner Close E4
Milton Street E7
Minerva Drive C5
Molteno Road D7
Monmouth Road E8
Moor View D10
Moss Road E4
Motorway (M1) F1-J8
Munden Grove F6
Muriel Avenue F10
Mutchetts Close G4, G3

N

Nancy Downs F11
Nascot Place E7
Nascot Road E7
Nascot Street E8, E7
Nascot Wood Road D6
Neal Street F9
Neston Road E6, F6
Nevill Grove E7
Newhouse Crescent E3
Newlands Walk F4
New Road F9
New Street E9
Nicholas Close E6
Norfolk Avenue F6
North Approach D4, E4
Northfield Gardens F6
North Obital Road D4-F3
North Western Avenue D5, E5
Nottingham Close E4

O

Oakdene Road E5
Oaklands Court D7
Occupational Road E9, E10
Old Forge Close D3, E3
Orbital Crescent D5
Orchard Avenue E3, E2
Orchard Close D7, D8
Orchard Drive D7
Orphanage Road D7, F8
Osborne Road F6
Otterspool Lane/Way G6
Oxford Street E9
Oxhey Avenue F11
Oxhey Road F10, F11

P

Park Avenue D8-E9
Park Road E7
Parker Street E7
Parkgate Road F6
Parkside Drive C8-E8
Pelhams, The F5, G5
Penn Road E7
Percy Road E9
Peregrine Close G4
Perivale Gardens E4
Phillipers G5, G4
Pinner Road F10, G10
Platts Avenue E8
Pomeroy Crescent E5
Pope's Lane E6
Polars Close E3
Poundfield D5
Pretoria Road E9
Princes Avenue D9
Prince Street F8
Purbrock Avenue E5, F5

Q

Queen Mary's Avenue C9
Queens Avenue D9
Queens Place F8
Queens Road F8, F9
Queenswood Crescent E3-E4

R

Radlett Road F8, F7
Redheath Close D4
Red Lion Yard E9, E8
Regent Street E6, E7
Rhodes Way F7
Richmond Drive C7
Rickmansworth Road C9-E8
Ridgehurst Avenue D4
Ridge Lane D6, D5
Ridge Street E6
Ridgeway, The C5-D6
Riverside Road E10
Robert Street F9
Rosebriar Walk D5
Rosecroft Drive C5
Rose Gardens E10
Ross Crescent D4, E4
Rosslyn Road E8
Rother Close F4
Roughwood Close C6
Roundway, The D10
Rowley Close
Rushton Avenue E5, E4
Russell Crescent D5
Russell Lane C5

S

St. Albans Road E8-G1
St. George's Road E6
St. James Road E9
St. John's Road E8
St. Mary's Close E9
St. Mary's Road E9
Salisbury Road E7
Sandown Road F6
Sandringham Road E6
Second Avenue F5, F4
Severn Way F4
Shady Lane E8
Shaftesbury Road F8
Shakespeare Close E6
Shakespeare Street E7
Sheepcot Drive F4
Sheepcot Lane E3-F4
Shepherds Road D8, D9
Sheridan Road F11
Sheriff Way E4
Sherwoods Road G11
Silverdell D5
Sixth Avenue F4
Smith Street F9
Sotheron Road F8
Souldern Street E9
Southfield Avenue F6
Southsea Avenue D9
Southwold Road F6
Spinney, The E7
Spring Gardens F5
Square, The E6
Stamford Road E7
Stanbury Avenue C6
Stanley Road F9
Stanmore Road E7
Station Approach D8, D9
Station Road E7-E8
Stones Alley E9
Strangeways C5
Stratford Road D8, E7
Stratford Way D8
Stud Green E3
Summerfield Road D4, D5
Sussex Road D6, E6
Sutton Road F8
Swiss Avenue C8
Swiss Close C8
Sycamore Close E4
Sydney Road C9, D9

T

Talbot Avenue G11
Tavistock Road F7
Telford Close F4, G4
Temple Close D7, D8
Terrace Gardens E7
Third Avenue F4, F5
Thorpe Crescent E11
Thrums, The E6
Tolpits Close D9, D10
Tolpits Lane B11-D11
Trefusis Walk C7
Trevellance Way F3, F4
Trident Road D4
Tucker Street F9
Tudor Avenue F6, G6
Tudor Drive F6, G6
Tudor Walk F6
Tunnel Wood Close D6
Tunnel Wood Road D6
Turnstones, The G5

U

Upper Paddock Road G10
Upton Road E9, E8

V

Valley Rise E3
Vicarage Road D10-E9
Victoria Road E7
Villiers Road G10

W

Walverns Close F10
Warneford Place G10
Water Lane F9
Waterman Close E10
Watford Field Road F9
Watford Heath F11
Watford Road B10-C9
Weall Green E3
Wellington Road E8
Wellstones E9
Wentworth Close D6
Westbury Road E9
West Drive E5
Westfield Avenue F6
Westland Road E8
Westlea Avenue G6, G5
* West Street E8
Whippendell Road C9-E9
Whitwell Road G5
Widgeon Way G6, G5
Wiggenhall Road E9, E10
Wilcot Avenue C11
Willow Lane E10
Wimborne Grove C6, C5
Windsor Road F6
Woodford Road E8, F8
Woodgate E3, E4
Woodhurst Avenue F4
Woodland Drive D7, D8
Woodmere Avenue C6
Woodside E5
Woodside Close E5
Woodside Road E2
Woodville Court D7
Woodwaye F11

Y

Yarmouth Road E7, F7
York Road F10
York Way G5

*This street no longer exists, but is shown on the map to indicate its former position.

Differing styles of street name plates

Top: the most general type with black lettering
on white enamel

Above left: the older style in cast iron. Black
lettering on a white background

Above right: the type put up in the Central area in
1972 to replace older ones destroyed by
road works. Also black lettering on
white enamel

Below: Sutton Road is another example of the older
cast iron type. Queen's Road is white lettering
on blue enamel. This is also an older type of
which few examples survive

Clifford & Gough plaques
Above left: Oxford Place, Gartlet Road
Above right: Banbury House, Queens Road
Below right: Herbert Terrace, Sutton Road
   Note the letters 'E.C.' standing for Edwin Clifford
Below left: Oxford Terrace, Westland Road

Above left: the statue of Queen Victoria on the wall
just below roof level at the junction of Pinner Road and
the south side of Grover Road
Above right: the large female figure high on the wall of
Clifford Street
Below: deep in Clifford & Gough territory. Souldern
Street showing a typical house built of yellow stock
bricks. There is a plaque and the date, plaque surround
and banding are in red bricks.

Above: Sutton Road. An interesting contrast between
the original plaque of Alma Terrace dated 1869 and a
simulated keystone put up to mark an improvement in 1963
Below: a closed shop in Estcourt Road serves as a striking
reminder of Watford's agricultural past

Above: Little Cassiobury, Hempstead Road. This now
houses the offices of the S.W. Herts Education Division
Below: Watford Place, King Street. This is now occupied
by the solicitors, Sedgwick, Turner, Sworder and Wilson

Above: Salters' Almshouses, Church Road
Below: the London Orphan Asylum, Orphanage Road
This is now offices for the Department of Employment

occurred on Lammas Day (August 1st) for grain lands and Old Midsummer Day (July 5th) for grass lands. They then remained open until the following Lady Day (March 25th).

LEA BUSHES see APPENDIX 3

LEANDER GARDENS see APPENDIX 2

LEAVESDEN ROAD   LEAVESDEN HIGH ROAD
This appears as Levesdenewode in 1333 and Levysdene in 1398. By 1504 it had become Levesden and there is mention of Levesdenwey, the road to Leavesden, in 1485. The word was probably derived from the proper name Leof and meant Leof's valley (denu).

LEGGATT'S CLOSE   LEGGATT'S RISE   LEGGATT'S WAY

LEGGATT'S WOOD AVENUE
Near both St. Paul's Walden and North Mimms the word 'Leggatts' occurs and is associated with a proper name. This is also true in Watford as mention is made in 1451 of a John Legat. From this source came Leggatt's Wood and Leggatt's Farm, which eventually gave the names of four roads and two schools, a record only equalled in the town by variations on Cassio and Cassiobury.

LEMON FIELD DRIVE see APPENDIX 3

LEVIATHAN ROAD see BEDFORD STREET

LIME AVENUE
Now is an opportune moment to record that this fine row of trees, which crosses the West Herts Golf Course from Cassiobury Park to Whippendell Woods, has reached the venerable age of 300 years. It was planted by Moses Cook, gardener to the 1st Earl of Essex, in November 1672. He relates, with justifiable pride, how, of the 296 trees raised by him at Hadham Hall, and transplanted from there to Cassiobury Park, he did not lose one within the first year.

LIME CLOSE see BROMET CLOSE

LINDEN LEA see APPENDIX 3

LIVERPOOL ROAD
The late nineteenth and early twentieth century was a boom period for Liverpool and its port became the largest in the country outside London. Its great series of docks had been almost completed and it possessed a fine collection of public buildings with the classical St. George's Hall as the most imposing. It was therefore logical that when a new road was constructed in 1895 to run out of Cardiff Road, it should be called by the name of this other great seaport.

LOATES LANE
This appears as Loft Lane in 1436 and Lofteslane in 1485, although what was the exact meaning is not clear. At one time it led from the High Street to Bushey Mill Lane, but its venerable age has been affronted by one original section being turned

into the present Radlett Road and a shorter stretch being renamed Queen's Place, so that it is now only a pale shadow of its former self.

LOCAL BOARD ROAD

Many towns in the North and Midlands have a Corporation Road and the beginning of municipal government, as we know it today, started with vestries followed by local boards of health. The Watford Local Board of Health which came into being in 1850 was housed in this small road at the end of the High Street near the River Colne and although it moved in 1892 to Upton House, in the High Street, its work is thus still commemorated. In the 1850's the thoroughfare was known simply as Board of Health Road.

LONG BARN CLOSE see APPENDIX 3

LONGCROFT see APPENDIX 3

LONGSPRING

An area of woodland running from near the present Gade Side to the St. Albans Road and joining on to Leggatt's Wood was called Longspring. At no point was it more than three hundred yards wide and it is interesting to note that a similar area of woodland on Grove Mill Lane is still called Deer Spring. The word 'spring' used in connection with woodland means a copse or grove consisting of trees springing up naturally from older growth and is also used for a plantation of young trees, especially one enclosed or used for rearing or keeping game. It would be reasonable to assume that deer were reared in both Deer Spring and Longspring, especially in view of the fact that Arthur Capel, when created Earl of Essex at the Restoration, obtained a licence to preserve game within ten miles of Cassiobury, and that herds of deer were kept at both Cassiobury and the Grove up to the early years of the twentieth century.

LOOSLEY'S CORNER

G. W. Loosley & Co. were booksellers and stationers at 114, High Street and these premises are now occupied by the tailors John Temple Ltd. The shop stands at the corner of an entrance to St. Mary's churchyard and thus became known as Loosley's Corner.

LOUVAIN WAY

The Belgian city of Louvain was sacked by the advancing Germans on August 25th 1914 on a pretext that the civilian population had joined in an attack on the occupying forces. The Church of St. Peter, the Law Courts, the Theatre, the Academy for Fine Arts and the University Library were destroyed and in the Treaty of Versailles, the Germans specifically agreed to make reparations for the lost books and manuscripts in the latter. When twenty-one years later in 1935, a street was being built off Horseshoe Lane, so vividly were the horrors of the First World War still remembered, that it would have been perfectly natural to name it Louvain Way to commemorate this anniversary of the town's destruction. Five years later in 1940, the advancing Germans again destroyed the new University Library in the town and it seems a sad commentary on man's folly, that the present

spirit of co-operation in Western Europe should have come about only after the monumental conflict of two world wars.

LOWER DERBY ROAD see ESTCOURT ROAD

LYCH GATE
Although this housing development in Garston dates only from 1962 a name of such venerable antiquity was obviously inspired by the proximity of All Saints Church. A lych gate formed the temporary resting place of a coffin while a funeral cortège was awaiting the arrival of the clergyman, but modern map-makers have shown a somewhat distressing tendency to change the name to 'Lynch Gate.' This seems to suggest that either the local population suffered an alarmingly accelerated mortality rate in the past or some sinister and as yet undetected force is at work in the present.

MALDEN ROAD see also DENMARK STREET
By letters patent dated April 20th 1661, Arthur Capel (1631-1683) was created Viscount Malden and Earl of Essex and in 1670, he was appointed Ambassador to the Court of Denmark, where 'he displayed great intrepidity in supporting the national character'. He was also Lord Lieutenant of Ireland from 1672 to 1677 and was arrested at Cassiobury in July 1683 for complicity in the Rye House Plot. He was lodged in the Tower of London, but on July 13th was found dead in his room with his throat cut and no satisfactory explanation of this tragic event has ever been given.

MANDEVILLE CLOSE
Geoffrey de Mandeville was a medieval landowner in the Manor of Cassio, whose name was used in July 1967 for a short street off Nascot Wood Road.

MARKET STREET see THE HIGH STREET

MAUDE CRESCENT
Sir Frederick Stanley Maude (1864-1917) was born at Gibraltar and was educated at Eton and Sandhurst. He joined the Coldstream Guards in 1884 and entered the Staff College at Camberley in 1895. During the Boer War he served with distinction and was awarded the D.S.O. He was military secretary to the Earl of Minto when the latter was Governor-General of Canada from 1901 to 1905 and from that latter date until the First World War, he had various staff appointments. On the outbreak of war he went first of all to France and then to the Dardanelles, where he took a prominent part in the evacuation from Suvla Bay and Helles. In 1916 he was put in command of the army in Mesopotamia, created K.C.B. and made a Lieutenant General. He was instrumental in securing the capture of both Kut and Baghdad, but died of cholera in the latter city. From the outbreak of war until his death he owned Mardale in Stratford Road, which is now used as an old people's home by the London Borough of Brent.

MEETING ALLEY see BEECHEN GROVE

MERIDEN WAY   MERIDEN ESTATE

Thirty years after the Norman Conquest the name Muridene was first recorded in 1097. By 1628 this had become Meriden and was chosen for the Borough Council's new housing estate when it was built in the area in the decade from 1957 to 1967. The variant form Munden occurs just outside the Borough at Munden House, the home of Lord Knutsford. The word comes from Old English and means 'at the pleasant valley.' The Holland-Hibbert family when elevated to the peerage took their title from Knutsford in Cheshire, the home town of the 1st Lord Knutsford. Thus Watford has Hibbert Avenue, Holland Gardens, Knutsford Avenue and Munden Grove as street names.

MERTON ROAD

The Masters and Fellows of Merton College, Oxford, owned land in the Market Street and Callowland areas of the town from at least 1380 onwards and this connection remained until 1881 when Callowland Farm was sold to the Earl of Essex and was subsequently developed for housing in the 1890's. A recent additional use of the name has been for the new Walter de Merton School in Gammon's Lane.

MICKEY MOUSE'S BUNGALOW

Next to the Central Library stands a large, rounded concrete construction, which looks like the entrance to a war-time operations room. It is an electricity substation and plans are afoot for its demolition in two or three years time. However, until that day dawns, it will still be known by engineers, who have anything to do with it, as Mickey Mouse's Bungalow.

MILDRED AVENUE

Mrs. Mildred Schreiber lived at Dalton House in the Lower High Street. The house was on the banks of the River Colne and the site is now occupied by the Ever Ready Battery Company. Mrs. Schreiber was one of the most prominent people in establishing the parish of St. Michael's, Durban Road, and many garden parties and pageants were held at Dalton House to raise money for this cause. The church was not consecrated until 1913, but Mildred Avenue was laid out in 1902 and even at this early stage in setting up the new parish, Mrs. Schreiber's efforts were recognised in this way.

MILTON STREET see also AYNHO STREET and CLIFTON ROAD

From visual evidence Milton Villa, a detached house in Milton Street, was almost certainly built by William Gough. Shakespeare Street runs out of Milton Street and both Milton and Shakespeare were sturdy Englishmen, who had none of the effete langour of Keats, the alarming revolutionary tendencies of Wordsworth or the morals of Byron, which were too awful to contemplate. Milton came from yeoman stock in Oxfordshire and Shakespeare was of course born in Stratford-on-Avon, so that in addition to their outstanding literary merit, they would also have satisfied William Gough's predilection for naming streets after midland associations connected with his youth. No less important is the fact that there are four villages in North Oxfordshire and South Northamptonshire called Milton. Great and Little Milton are just east of Oxford, Milton Malsor is five miles south

west of Northampton and most significant of all, there is one just called Milton five miles west of Aynho, William Gough's birthplace. Byron had the last laugh however, and is commemorated by Byron Avenue, which was built and named in 1938, presumably to celebrate the 150th anniversary of his birth in 1788, and by that date his morals, far from being a liability, had become a positive asset.

MINERVA DRIVE see APPENDIX 4

MOLTENO ROAD

The houses in this road were built in 1968 for occupation by naval personnel and it was named after Captain V. B. Molteno, who commanded H.M.S. Warrior, an armoured cruiser of 13,750 tons, which was sunk at the Battle of Jutland.

MONK'S FOLLY LANE see WIGGENHALL ROAD

MONMOUTH ROAD

Sir Robert Carey was created Earl of Monmouth and came to live at Moor Park, Rickmansworth, in the early 1600's. He built a house which was referred to in the deeds as his 'Mansion House' on the north side of Watford High Street near the pond. During the eighteenth and nineteenth centuries it was altered and divided in two, one part being called Monmouth House and the other The Platts after the ancestral home in Worcestershire of the Cox family, who lived there for generations. Both houses were again altered to present a uniform facade when they were converted to business premises in 1927.

THE MOUNT see GREENCROFT CRESCENT

MUNDEN GROVE see MERIDEN WAY

NANCY DOWNS see APPENDIX 3

NASCOT AVENUE see THE AVENUE

NASCOT PLACE, see also TUKE or TUKE'S ROAD or STREET

NASCOT ROAD   NASCOT STREET   NASCOT WOOD ROAD

In 1436 this was Nascotte and in 1556 Nascott meades. It appears that this came from the Middle English atten ast cote meaning at the east cote. A cot or cote was a stall or shelter for animals, especially sheep and was also used for domestic fowl such as hens and doves. By the nineteenth century this area had become the Nascot Wood Estate and in 1857 was being described as 'A fine tract of land comprising about one hundred and fifty acres, lying between the railway and the High Road to Hemel Hempstead on which it has a frontage of about 1600 yards. Its nearest point to the Watford Station is one fifth of a mile and its most distant is one mile.' [10] From the 1850's onwards the Estate was being developed as a residential area to encourage the middle and professional classes to work in London and with the aid of the railway live in the country. Somewhat earlier, south of the Thames, John Ruskin's father, who was a wine merchant in the City, had taken a house at Herne Hill in 1823 and moved to one on Denmark Hill in 1842, which he occupied until his death in 1864. John Ruskin himself in Praeterita (p.47)

described the almost arcadian delights of the undeveloped Herne Hill of his youth and it was the stage coach and turnpike roads, which started modern commuting as we know it, [11] a process which the railways accelerated very rapidly. Herne Hill, Denmark Hill and many similar districts have now been swallowed by London, but in spite of modern building, the present Nascot Wood estate still retains to a very marked degree the feel of 'rus in urbe'.

NEAL STREET and TUCKER STREET

NESTON ROAD
Neston and Parkgate are two small towns in the Wirral of Cheshire. Neston was the birthplace of Emma, Lady Hamilton, while during the eighteenth century, Parkgate was the port of departure for the Irish packet. Handel sailed from the port in 1741 to give the first performance of the 'Messiah' in Dublin and made last minute corrections to the score there before embarking. I have not been able to trace the reason for the use of these two names in Watford, but it seems not unreasonable to suppose that whoever developed the two roads had family connections with the towns or an affection for them.

NEW ROAD   NEW STREET
In many towns there is a New Road or Street, which on examination turns out to be one of the oldest thoroughfares and is shown on the earliest maps. Watford is no exception as mention is made of la Neustrete in 1436 in the Court Rolls of the Manor of Cassiobury. Visitors to the Church Street multi-storey car park adjacent to New Street may be forgiven however, if they think that the name dates from the time the car park was built. New Road, if not equally venerable, is still one of the oldest thoroughfares in Watford.

NEWHOUSE CRESCENT
In 1594 there is reference to le newe house which in time became Newhouse Farm and is shown as such just south of Horseshoe Lane on the 1871 Ordnance Survey map.

NICHOLAS CLOSE see BREAKSPEARE CLOSE

NORFOLK AVENUE   NORFOLK ROAD see BRUCE GROVE

NORTH-WESTERN AVENUE see THE BY-PASS

NOTTINGHAM CLOSE see SHERWOODS ESTATE

OAKLANDS COURT see APPENDIX 4

OCCUPATION ROAD
This is a term often employed for a private right of way which is used by the occupants of houses in a road. There was an Occupation Cottage which stood here until demolished in 1962 and it is worth recording that it still remains a private road and has never been adopted by the Borough Council.

ORPHANAGE ROAD

The London Orphan Asylum was founded at Clapton in 1813, but after a bout of cholera there was some haste to change its location and the Prince of Wales laid the foundation stone for a new range of buildings in Watford in 1869. The opening ceremony was performed in 1871 by Princess Mary of Cambridge, Duchess of Teck, and orphans from professional, commercial and service families were accommodated there. The buildings are at present occupied by the Department of Employment. The whole of the approach road from the St. Albans Road to the Orphanage was originally called Asylum Road but presumably on the principle that orphans should be neither seen nor heard, the section from the St. Albans Road to the junction of Woodford and Queen's Roads was renamed St. John's Road, even though St. John's Church was built in Sutton Road. Now only a very short stretch either side of the railway bridge forms the present Orphanage Road.

OSBORNE ROAD see BALMORAL ROAD

OTTERSPOOL LANE   OTTERSPOOL WAY

As the name implies, this was once a pool which was the haunt of otters and had several springs welling up from the deepest parts of it. It was later included in the grounds of the eighteenth century Great Otterspool House, which stands on the east side of the River Colne by the Berrygrove Roundabout. The House has been considerably altered and in the latter half of the nineteenth century was owned by Sidney Taprell Holland. A previous owner, Judge Willis, took a vast quantity of broken crockery, ginger-beer, soda water and champagne bottles from the River Colne at this point, as the building had formerly been a fashionable hotel and had attracted parties from London seeking entertainment. At present the House is used as a residence for Wall Hall Training College. At the point where Water Lane crosses the river Colne there was another pool known as Little Otterspool.

OTTOMAN TERRACE

From the 1840's onwards, the Ottoman Empire was looked upon as a buffer state against the encroaching might of Imperial Russia and during the Crimean War the Turks were allies of Britain and France. However, after 1856 the position gradually changed and relations between Britain and the Ottoman Empire deteriorated to the point where the latter threw in its lot with the Central Powers during the First World War. One of the turning points in this relationship was the Turkish Massacre of 12,000 Bulgarians in 1876, an event which caused Gladstone to publish his famous pamphlet entitled 'The Bulgarian Horrors and the Question of the East,' in which he called for the removal of the Turks from Bulgaria 'bag and baggage.' With this historical background in mind, it is ironic that Ottoman Terrace should run parallel to Gladstone Road, although the main Euston line passes between them to keep the peace.

OXHEY AVENUE   OXHEY ROAD

This appears to have been derived from a word meaning an enclosure or fenced-in place for oxen rather like a Central African boma. The area appears to have been granted to the Abbey of St. Albans by King Offa about 790 (although there is doubt

about the authenticity of the Charter) and the good monks would have doubtless been keen to keep their own oxen from straying and to prevent thieves stealing them. At this very early date there would also have been danger of attack by wolves, although it is not widely known that by the Middle Ages they had been exterminated in England and thus the great sheep-runs of Gloucestershire, Yorkshire and East Anglia were developed and created the wealth that produced the large wool-churches of these areas.

PARKGATE ROAD see NESTON ROAD

THE PELHAMS see APPENDIX 2

PERCY ROAD
In May 1455 Henry VI accompanied by Percy, Earl of Northumberland, and two thousand men stayed the night in Watford on their way to meet the Duke of York and the Earl of Warwick at the Battle of St. Albans. In addition the Earls of Essex were related to the Earls of Northumberland by marriage. However, when the road was laid out in 1891 it was not these historic links that determined its name, but the fact that Frank Fisher, a well-known local butcher, had decided to put money into land development and had both Percy and Francis Road called after his two sons. Frank Fisher himself was Chairman of the Watford Urban District Council from 1901-1903 and was Chairman of the committee, which was arranging the local celebrations for King Edward VII's coronation in 1902. When the King became acutely ill with appendicitis, the celebrations were cancelled and this led to riots, in which Frank Fisher's shop and others were attacked and stoned.

PEST HOUSE LANE see WILLOW LANE

PHILLIPERS see APPENDIX 3

PLATT'S AVENUE see MONMOUTH ROAD

POE LANE or POE FIELDS LANE see SHADY LANE

POPE'S LANE see BREAKSPEARE CLOSE

PRETORIA ROAD see DURBAN ROAD

PRINCE STREET see DUKE STREET

PURBROCK AVENUE
This came from the telescoping and slight alteration of two names. One was that of an estate agent called Perry and the other of a builder called Brockett.

QUEEN'S PLACE see LOATES LANE

QUEEN'S ROAD
When this road was being constructed north of the High Street in the early 1860's, it was natural to name it after Queen Victoria, as even by that date her reign was approaching its silver jubilee. In the early years, the section nearest the High Street seems to have been called Queen Street as often as Queen's Road. It originally went

as far as Loates Lane but the section north of Derby Road is now known as the Broadway.

RADLETT ROAD see LOATES LANE

REDHEATH CLOSE see APPENDIX 2

REGENT STREET
This street was named by William Judge, who had a fondness for Regent Street in London, but it must surely have been more than blind chance that put it next to Victoria Road and in close proximity to Brighton and Sussex Roads. In the most unlikely event of this selection of street names ever having come to the notice of the Queen, she would certainly not have been amused, as she had the gravest doubts about the morals of her wicked uncle and certainly evinced no enthusiasm whatsoever for the Royal Pavilion, which was sold to the town of Brighton in 1850.

RHODES WAY see COLONIAL WAY

RICHMOND DRIVE
When the Cassiobury estate was being laid out in the 1930's, it was felt that either Sir Richard or Sir Charles Morrison Avenue would be a suitable street name, as it was the grand-daughter of the latter, Elizabeth Morrison, who married a member of the Capel family and thus brought Cassiobury to the Earls of Essex. However, on more mature reflection, it was felt to be too long a name and Richmond Drive was substituted, as this denoted a leafy and pleasant part of what was then Surrey and has now become just another part of the Metropolis.

RICKMANSWORTH ROAD
The road to Rickmansworth is one of the four that formed the cross-roads in the centre of Watford and goes back to the earliest history of the town. From 1770 to 1881 it was part of the Reading to Hatfield Turnpike Trust and until the early 1900's formed the southern boundary of the Cassiobury Estate.

RIDGE LANE   RIDGE STREET   RIDGEWAY
The present Ridge Lane follows faithfully the line of the former bridle way that ran from opposite Ridge Lane Lodge on the Hempstead Road to Gammon's Lane and Gammon's Farm, and the Ridgeway was a logical extension of the use of the name. Ridge Street however, has nothing to do with either. Reginald Judge, the son of William Judge the builder, was known in the family as 'Ridge' and not 'Reg' and used to sign his name this way on occasions. It was therefore this nickname and not any local topographical feature that gave Watford Ridge Street.

RIVERSIDE ROAD see ROOKERY ROAD

ROBERTS ROAD
Piet Cronje was one of the principal Boer generals in the South African War and played a prominent part in the siege of Mafeking. The relief of this town rejoiced the hearts of Britons out of all proportion to its actual military value. The name of Cronje had become so well-known because of this event, that when a road was laid

out in 1902 between Tucker and Neal Streets, it was named after him. However, by the end of the same year, this magnanimity towards a former enemy had entirely evaporated and the road was renamed in somewhat unseemly haste after Field Marshal Lord Roberts, the hero of the hour, who apart from having gained the V.C. for his conduct during the Indian Mutiny and distinguished himself in Afghanistan, had also brought about the final victory in South Africa at a time when several European powers were considering whether to side with the Boers. Lord Roberts was in addition a resident of Abbots Langley and on October 1st 1902 opened a charity bazaar in Watford at the Clarendon Hall. No doubt the change was greeted with relief by the postal authorities, for whom a simple British name was far less likely to cause problems, than one that most people would have found difficult to pronounce and spell.

ROOKERY ROAD
Rookery Road led to the Rookery Silk Mill in the nineteenth century, but on the building of the Wiggenhall estate in the 1930's, the name was changed to Riverside Road. Perhaps like the alteration of Pest House Lane to Willow Lane, this is another example of what Eric Partridge in his book Usage and Abusage called a 'genteelism', as a rookery was a common slang term for a slum. The name still survives undiminished however in the popular 'Rookery End' of the Watford Football Club's ground in Vicarage Road.

ROSS CRESCENT see THORPE CRESCENT

ROUGHWOOD CLOSE
Rough Wood was a small area of woodland about 150 yards square that stood between Ridge Lane Lodge on the Hempstead Road and the Grand Junction (now Grand Union) Canal. The present Roughwood Close was built partially on the same site.

ROUSEBARN LANE
In the eighteenth century this was Rose Barn Lane and probably came from Henry Rowce, who in 1527 had been party to a deed concerning a messuage in Watford. It remains to this day a delightful, narrow country lane, which has contrived miraculously to survive intact so close to a large urban area.

RUSHTON AVENUE see THORPE CRESCENT

ST. ALBANS ROAD
St. Albans was one of the most important cities in the country in Roman times, many hundreds of years before Watford had any recorded history. Watford is now the larger of the two towns, but St. Albans has the cathedral of the diocese, which was only established in 1877, although the building itself is medieval and incorporates large quantities of re-used Roman bricks and tiles. The road connecting the two towns has always been an important route across South-West Hertfordshire and the Watford end is an important shopping centre. Like many other ancient roads of the country, it is now forced to pass humbly beneath that twentieth century upstart, the M.1.

ST. JAMES' ROAD

This is one of the most puzzling roads in the whole of Watford. It appears to have been named after the mission church of St. James, Watford Fields, which was situated in Lammas Road and was superseded by the present building erected in 1913. The road itself was laid out in 1893 and developed from 1895, while Lammas Road dates from 1891. It is highly confusing to have a street named after a church, which is elsewhere, and this confusion is compounded by the fact that there is a Church in the road dating from 1904. This is St. James' *Road* Baptist Church, a modern building which has replaced an earlier one on the same site. Perhaps the explanation lies in the great wave of anglican and non-conformist piety which swept through late Victorian and Edwardian England and would have made it quite natural at the time to highlight one of the many mission churches of the day. A glance at the publicity material in a contemporary local directory shows that there must have been a brisk trade in tin tabernacles, for sandwiched between advertisements for money to relieve lost and starving dogs, blouses with a tightness at the waist that would have made the wearers soon completely deformed and a whole page extolling the virtues of Cobra—*the* boot polish, which shows a snake in top hat, wing collar and bow tie being buffed up by two monkeys, one of which is wearing a fez, there is one splendid example offering for sale new and *second-hand* churches. Apparently with these metal masterpieces in the best Gothic style you could also, if you were unwise enough, procure '100 tons of iron free on application.' The First World War brought developments of this kind to an abrupt end and many of these buildings were given a new and honourable lease of life as cricket pavilions and village halls. One other curious fact remains to be recorded. There is a house in the road called Aston Villa when every football enthusiast knows that Newcastle United plays at St. James' Park.

ST. JOHN'S ROAD see ORPHANAGE ROAD

ST. MICHAEL'S AVENUE

This appeared as a proposed road on a sale plan of 1909 and was to have been built parallel to and east of Shepherd's Road and would have joined Cassiobury Park Avenue to the Rickmansworth Road at a point opposite Harwoods Road. The name was obviously derived from St. Michael's Church, Durban Road. The Church was not consecrated until 1913, but advance preparations for its building were well in hand by 1909.

SALISBURY ROAD see CECIL STREET

SALTERS' ALMSHOUSES

For many years there was confusion in the town between Salters' Almshouses in Church Road built by the City Livery Company of that name and Salter's Almshouses in the High Street near Watford Field Road. These latter were provided by a local benefactor, David Salter, and have now been demolished, thus neatly solving the problem.

SANDRINGHAM ROAD see BALMORAL ROAD

SECOND AVENUE see APPENDIX 3

SHADY LANE

Featherbed Lane was a bridleway which led from a point near the junction of Clarendon Road and the High Street to the bridge over the railway on the St. Albans Road. Like some of the lanes of Devonshire, part of it was sunk below the level of surrounding fields and had high banks on which there was a good deal of undergrowth and also larger trees, principally elms, that gave shade to passers-by. On a hot summer's day with all the foliage out, the total effect must have been completely soporific, and it would be pleasing to think that this was the reason for the name. However, it was also a field name in the area and would have denoted a piece of badly drained land, which in wet weather became miry and difficult to work and was thus a 'featherbed.' The character of the bridleway made it natural that people should think of it at night as being the haunt of ghosts and evil spirits, and when the whole area was developed for housing, the short road between Clarendon and Westland Roads was called Shady Lane, probably as a reminder of its past. It is interesting to note in this connection, that to local people, the word 'shady' would have the double connotation of a place in shadow that by inference was the haunt of underhand or unpleasant happenings. It has long since lost its former notoriety and become very law-abiding, as it now houses one frontage of the present main police station. Part of Featherbed Lane also appears to have been known as Poe Lane or Poe Fields Lane as this was another field name in the area. The footpath that runs from Station Road along the side of the Clarendon Hotel and back to the St. Albans Road is still known simply as the Bridlepath.

SHAKESPEARE STREET see MILTON STREET

SHEEPCOT DRIVE   SHEEPCOT LANE

Whether the rolling English drunkard made the rolling English road or vice versa was a problem posed by G. K. Chesterton and one which the meandering progress of Sheepcot Lane seems specifically designed to emphasise. It was originally a country lane leading to a sheepcot or sheepcote, a shelter or stall for sheep, and has suffered the indignity of being cut into halves by North Western Avenue.

SHEPHERD'S ROAD

Until 1956 Shepherd's or Thorn Cottage stood in what are now the grounds of the Grammar School for Boys at the junction of the west side of Shepherd's Road and the north side of the Rickmansworth Road. It was formerly one of the lodges to the Cassiobury Estate and had been used to house shepherds who worked there.

SHERIFF WAY see SHERWOODS ESTATE

SHERWOODS ESTATE   SHERWOODS ROAD

Sherwoods seems originally to have been a corruption of 'Shire wood' and the word shire itself in medieval times was used for a piece of land owned by an abbey or within ecclesiastical jurisdiction of some kind. Gradually the meaning was widened to cover larger stretches of land the size of the present counties, and because Sherwood Forest in Nottinghamshire was so extensive, it became the outstanding

example of a wood within a shire. Due south of Watford Heath there is an area of woodland called Sherwoods Wood and this was the origin of Sherwoods Road. At the other end of the Borough the new Corporation housing estate being built on the north side of the North Orbital Road opposite the Kingswood estate is to be called the Sherwoods estate after Samuel Sherwood, who is mentioned in the Tithe Apportionment of 1844. Three of the streets on the estate however, Forest Road, Nottingham Close and Sheriff Way revert to associations with Sherwood Forest, while a fourth, Haines Way, commemorates Councillor Laurance Haines, Mayor of Watford during 1951/52.

SHRODELLS

This seems to have been a contracted form of shrubbery dell, but far from having neat little shrubs, it is likely to have been a hollow covered with brushwood and rough undergrowth, in fact, just the kind of area to appeal to the builders of the workhouse, when they were looking for a site. Parts of this latter building are now included in the present modern Shrodells Hospital.

THE SHRUBBERY (Multi-storey car park) see APPENDIX 4

SILVER DELL see APPENDIX 4

SIR RICHARD MORRISON AVENUE see RICHMOND DRIVE

SIXTH AVENUE see APPENDIX 3

SMITH STREET see KING STREET

SOTHERON ROAD see ESTCOURT ROAD

SPARROWPOT LODGES

A sparrow pot or bottle was a jar suspended on a wall to serve as a nesting place for sparrows. Lest it be thought that this was merely a piece of eighteenth or nineteenth century altruism, it should be added that there were also at that time numerous recipes in which small birds figured prominently. The two Sparrowpot lodges to the Cassiobury Estate no longer exist, but used to stand until just after the Second World War on the south side of Grove Mill Lane at the eastern edge of Whippendell Woods.

STAMFORD ROAD see APPENDIX 4

STANBOROUGH PARK

In 1348 this was Stanburghehulle, probably meaning 'stone hill', a name which also occurs at Hatfield. The large late Victorian house called the Stanboroughs was built in about 1890 and from 1912 to 1968 was used as a hydro and nursing home. In 1906 the whole Park was bought by the Seventh Day Adventist Church and buildings were erected for headquarters purposes. At the time of writing the Church still owns the Park and although there has been talk of its sale it appears unlikely to become available for development.

STANBURY AVENUE see APPENDIX 4

STANLEY ROAD see ESTCOURT ROAD

STONE'S ALLEY
In 1888, a butcher's shop was demolished to provide an entrance to Market Street and this shop had formerly belonged to George Stone. The alley at the side of the shop led to Charles Moore's saleyard. Owing to recent development in the area, the part of the alley from the High Street to Exchange Road has suffered a kind of municipal cannibalisation and been combined with Well's Yard to form a new street called 'Wellstones.' From Exchange Road to Cassio Road however, the alley retains its original name.

STUD GREEN see APPENDIX 3

SUSSEX ROAD see REGENT STREET

SUTTON ROAD see ESTCOURT ROAD

SWISS AVENUE   SWISS CLOSE
The Cassiobury Estate possessed a cottage built in the style of a large Swiss chalet and it was used for occupation by a family, but also for open-air parties, fetes and sports gatherings. It became ruinous and was destroyed by fire in the Second World War, possibly through the carelessness of somebody sleeping rough on the premises. Popular opinion still has it that Cassiobridge Lodge at the junction of Gade Avenue and the Rickmansworth Road is the original Swiss Cottage, because of a superficial resemblance in construction, and it is doubtful whether this folk myth will ever die.

TEMPLE CLOSE
Temple Cottage stood on the Hempstead Road opposite the entrance to Langley Road at what is now the present junction of Langley Way and the Hempstead Road and the name was transferred to the present Temple Close.

THIRD AVENUE see APPENDIX 3

THOMAS'S CORNER
On the north corner of the junction of Harwoods and Holywell Roads stands a shop (No. 13) once occupied by a shopkeeper called Thomas and the name has survived to the present. An official street name plate is still over the doorway to No. 13, which now houses a dress agency.

THORPE CRESCENT
It is common throughout the country to honour elected members of the local authority by means of streets named after them. This is the reason for Thorpe and Ross Crescents, Bridger, Goodrich and Gorle Closes, Rushton and Evans Avenues and Clarke, Coates and Hemming Ways. Alderman Ralph Thorpe was Chairman of the Urban District Council on four separate occasions from 1904 to 1919 and Mayor of Watford from 1923 to 1925 after the incorporation of the Borough in 1922. Councillor Walter Goodrich was Chairman of the Urban District Council from 1913 to 1915 and Councillor Frederick Gorle from 1919 to 1920. Alderman

Thomas Rushton was Mayor of Watford from 1927 to 1928, Alderman Francis Hemming from 1928 to 1930, Alderman Joseph Evans from 1932 to 1933, Alderman Henry Bridger from 1934 to 1935, his wife Alderman Mrs. Mary Bridger from 1950 to 1951 and Alderman Henry Coates from 1936 to 1937 and again from 1947 to 1949. Councillors J. Ross and W. Clarke were also honoured by having streets named after them, although they never became Mayors and in 1971 part of Cow Lane was changed to York Way in memory of Councillor 'Bert' York. In addition, William Hudson who was Clerk to the Urban District Council from 1910 to 1922 and Town Clerk after the incorporation of the Borough from 1922 to 1940, is also commemorated by Hudson Close.

THRUMS
Thrums are the fringe of threads left on a loom when the web has been cut off and readers of J. M. Barrie's works will recall his use of the word as a small Scottish town in his sketch A Window in Thrums. However, a Ralph Trum is mentioned in a 1438 Patent Roll and the likely explanation is that the word used here is a corruption of his name and has nothing whatever to do with weaving.

TOLPITS LANE
This appears in 1365 as Tolpade, which had become Tollepathe by 1529 with mention of Tolpott bridge in 1594. It seems to have been some form of toll path with the 'pit' a modern corruption, but all trace of a toll being exacted in this area has long since vanished. There was also a farm in the area and in the eighteenth century provided Tolpulls as another variant in the form of the name.

TOWN HAMLET see the HIGH STREET

TREFUSIS WALK
Trefusis Point and House are on the west side of Falmouth Harbour and there is a strong tradition in Watford that the daughter of a former owner of this property married a member of the family of the Earls of Essex. I can find no documentary support for this theory, but it has given Watford an unusual and pleasing street name.

TRIDENT ROAD see COMET CLOSE

TUCKER STREET see BIRCH ROAD

TUDOR AVENUE   TUDOR DRIVE   TUDOR WALK
Between the two world wars a nostalgia for the greatness of the England of Elizabeth I overcame architects and builders and houses in the Tudor style appeared all over the country. These three roads were largely the work of the building firm of Rice Brothers and are the outstanding examples of the style in Watford.

TUKE or TUKE'S ROAD or STREET
By 1890 Nascot Place had acquired its present name but up to at least 1877 it was known as Tuke or Tuke's Road or Street. This strongly suggests that Tuke was a former property owner in the street or that it was built on his land. The name was presumably changed either because he sold his property holding or he died and the houses passed into other hands.

TUMBLING BAY
This picturesque name appears on the 1871 Ordnance Survey map for the stretch of the river Colne beside the weir, opposite what is now the western end of Oxhey Park and Riverside Road. The present overhead power lines rather spoil this romantic image, which is reminiscent of the Scottish lochs and Swiss mountain streams, so widely portrayed in steel engravings of the Victorian period. These latter were usually well supplied with shaggy highland cattle or groups of the sure-footed ibex and their popularity may be traced to the vogue for continental holidays made so much easier by the globe-trotting Thomas Cook, ably aided and abetted by the Germanic thoroughness of the guide books produced by the formidable and indefatigable Karl Baedeker.

UNION STREET see VICARAGE ROAD

UPTON ROAD see APPENDIX 4

VICARAGE ROAD
This is probably the best known Watford street name in the rest of the country, not as a result of its original ecclesiastical connection, but because it houses the ground of the Watford Football Club, known affectionately as 'The Hornets.' Due to changes in the modern street pattern in the centre of the town, Vicarage Road no longer actually contains St. Mary's Vicarage, but stops short at Exchange Road. During at least the first half of the nineteenth century, the western end of the road was known loosely as Union Street because of the hated workhouse (now part of Shrodells Hospital) situated there.

VICTORIA ROAD see REGENT STREET

VILLIERS ROAD see HYDE ROAD

WARNEFORD PLACE
Reginald Warneford was born at Darjeeling and was the son of a civil engineer. On the outbreak of the First World War, he joined The Royal Fusiliers and in 1915 transferred to the Royal Naval Air Service. On June 7th of that same year while flying between Bruges and Ghent, he dropped six bombs onto a Zeppelin and set it on fire. The force of the resultant explosion turned his aircraft upside down, but he managed to land safely in enemy territory. With consummate coolness, he was able to start the engine again, and return to his aerodrome. For this feat he was awarded the V.C. and it was largely as a result of his daring, that the authorities first realized how vulnerable Zeppelins were. Only ten days after his famous exploit, he was killed when his machine broke up in mid-air and so became one of the millions of the 'lost generation', who did not survive the hostilities and about whom Wilfred Owen wrote in his poem 'The Send-Off'.

> Shall they return to beatings of great bells
> In wild train-loads?
> A few, a few, too few for drums and yells,
> May creep back, silent, to village wells
> Up half-known roads.

This had a prophetic ring as Owen himself was killed in action on November 4th 1918, a week before the Armistice. Warneford had only the tenuous link with Watford of paying frequent visits to friends in Oxhey, but this seems unimportant compared with the knowledge that after more than half a century, this road in the town still keeps alive the memory of a very brave man.

WARREN AVENUE see GREENCROFT CRESCENT

WATERFIELD ESTATE see BUTCHER'S ESTATE

WATERMAN CLOSE see ASHBY ROAD

WATFORD
A great deal of ink has been spilt over the name of the original small settlement that grew up at the point where the river Colne could be crossed by a ford and the following are a selection of the more ingenious.
Wetford. A deep ford that wetted the traveller.
Wadeford. A ford which you could normally wade across.
Wattleford. A ford that had a protective screen of wattles.
Watlingford. A ford on the branch of the Roman Watling Street.
Wata's ford. A ford named after a local Saxon chieftain.
What ford is that? A passing dignitary is supposed to have made this remark, an endearing explanation that has all the qualities of a folk myth based on no shred of evidence whatsoever.
The weakness of all these suggestions is that none seems to be in the least plausible. Anybody crossing a ford must get wet and have to wade when the river is in spate. Wattles could hardly form any protection for a river crossing and would merely impede the flow of water. Watling Street crossed a great many rivers and it is unlikely that a crossing of the Colne on this obscure branch of the main highway would have been dignified by being named Watlingford, while no documentary evidence exists for a Saxon called Wata.
The more likely explanation is that 'Wat' comes from the Old English 'wath' meaning 'hunting' and that this was a ford used regularly by men out hunting, especially as the surrounding heavily wooded countryside would have been ideal for such activity.

WATFORD FIELD ROAD see FARTHING LANE

WELLINGTON ROAD see CANTERBURY ROAD

WELLSTONES see STONE'S ALLEY

WEST STREET
No street denoting one of the cardinal points of the compass existed in medieval Watford and when a short street was built in the 1850's it was named West Street, in all probability quite simply because it was the west side of the St. Albans Road.

WESTBURY ROAD see CLIFTON ROAD

WESTLAND ROAD see CANTERBURY ROAD

WESTLEA AVENUE see APPENDIX 2

WEYMOUTH STREET see also ALBERT ROAD and CANTERBURY ROAD

This was a street that was gradually done to death. In its heyday it stretched from the St. Albans Road, along what is now Albert Road and as far as what is now the southern half of Westland Road. The Albert Road/Westland Road section was called Weymouth Road North and the reason for the change in name is made clear under the entries for Albert Road and Canterbury Road. In spite of this drastic surgery, Weymouth Street survived for almost another century and was only finally given its quietus by the phase of the Central Area Development Plan started in 1970. Although the name has gone, it leaves a mystery behind. It would seem highly likely that a Watford builder had family and business connections in Weymouth or at least a fondness for the resort, as there is a Cassiobury Street in the latter town. This could hardly have been named by chance, nor was the land on which it was built owned by the Earls of Essex. In spite of extensive enquiries, I have not been able to reach any conclusions except that Weymouth Street in Watford was built about ten or fifteen years earlier than Cassiobury Street in Weymouth, so it can be reasonably assumed that pleasure or family ties come before business interests.

WHEATSHEAF ORCHARD

Wheatsheaf Cottages stood in a small street called Wheatsheaf Orchard, which ran back towards the river Colne from the south side of the High Street, almost at its junction with Chalk Hill and Eastbury Road. The street survived as an entry in Peacock's Directory until 1926, although after 1910 nobody seemed to think it worthwhile including it on the accompanying map. The public house called the Wheatsheaf in the High Street near this point still recalls this pleasantly rural name.

WHIPPENDELL ROAD   WHIPPENDELL WOODS

The first appearance of the name was in 1333 as Whippedenfeld. This became Whippedene in 1364, Whyppenden in 1390, Whependen Grove in 1545 and Whippenden Bottom in 1607. It appears to come from the personal name Wippa combined with denu, a valley (with dell often replacing denu), and thus Wippa's valley. There are several similar examples in other parts of the country.

WHITWELL ROAD see APPENDIX 2

WIGGENHALL ROAD

Wiggen Hall was a large house occupied among notable owners by several generations of the Deacon family and also Jonathan King. There has been a variety of spelling ranging from Wygenhale in the fourteenth century to Wyggynhalle in 1505 and Wythinghall in 1556. The first part of the word may be connected with an Old English word meaning 'withy' and this accords with the fact that the area is low-lying. There was also a Wiggenhall Bridge, which was the private property of T. F. Blackwell and led to Oxhey Place. It was demolished in 1925 to make way for a modern bridge when the road was taken over as a public highway. In the

Middle Ages a lane called Monk's Folly ran from here northward towards the Rickmansworth Road roughly along the line of the present Cassio Road. The modern English word 'folly' seemed to have been derived from several sources, which have now become thoroughly entangled. Two early French words, 'folie' meaning 'foolishness' and 'feuillie' meaning a leafy bower or forest clearing, were often confused. In Middle English 'folie' denoted a position taken up by a shooter of game. In Berkshire and Wiltshire 'folly' often means a clump of trees on top of a hill or open ground. As the whole area appears to have been granted by King Offa to the Abbey of St Albans about 790 (although there is doubt about the authenticity of the Charter), it seems likely that this use of 'folly' merely indicates wooded land in the Abbey's possession, although it would be pleasing to think of some now long forgotten band of monks constructing an ingenious but splendidly useless tower or pyramid, itself long since vanished. What is now Farraline Road was part of Wiggenhall Road until 1898 and was named after a house called Farraline.

WILLOW LANE
This is an example of what Eric Partridge in his book Usage and Abusage would have dubbed a 'genteelism' or an 'elegance', as the road was originally called Pest House Lane and in it stood the Pest House where smallpox victims were taken. Such a constant reminder of human mortality finally became too much and the present more salubrious name was substituted.

WINDSOR ROAD see BALMORAL ROAD

WOODFORD ROAD
Sir Alexander George Woodford (1782-1870) went to Winchester and afterwards had a distinguished army career. He took part in the bombardment and investment of Copenhagen in 1807, served in Sicily, the Mediterranean, the Peninsular War and also at Waterloo. After the Congress of Vienna in 1815 he held various military and administrative appointments and became Lieutenant-Governor of Chelsea Hospital in 1856. He succeeded to the Governorship on the death of Sir Edward Blakeney in 1868, when he was created a Field Marshal, and it was in the same year that Woodford Road was laid out in Watford.

WOODLANDS PARADE see APPENDIX 4

WOODMERE AVENUE
This is a pleasing portmanteau word inspired by the nearby Otterspool and Berrygrove Wood, now reduced to a few shivering silver birches by the roundabout at the junction of the M.1. and the A.41. Otterspool has undergone a romantic Tennysonian transformation into the mere of the Morte D'Arthur during the process of coining the name.

> So flash'd and fell the brand Excalibur
> But ere he dipt the surface, rose an arm
> Clothed in white samite, mystic, wonderful,
> And caught him by the hilt, and brandish'd him
> Three times, and drew him under in the mere.

WOODSIDE   WOODSIDE CLOSE

When the Harebreaks estate was built two roads on the south and east sides of the Harebreaks recreation ground were named Woodside and Woodside Close, presumably because they were at the edge of the former area of woodland called Longspring. When the Corporation housing estate was built after the Second World War in the area between the North Orbital Road, Horseshoe Lane and Leavesden High Road it was also called Woodside, but this was after an original name for the land around and there was also a house called Woodside Lodge near the present Farmer Close and Woodgate.

WOODVILLE COURT see APPENDIX 4

YE CORNER

This is a piece of fake antiquarianism, as the name does not date from medieval times, but was only bestowed on a new row of shops and commercial premises at the corner of Chalk Hill and Aldenham Road by an enterprising builder in 1907.

YORK ROAD

This road was laid out in 1891 and 1892, and in the latter year Prince George, later to become George V, was created Duke of York on the untimely death of his brother, the Duke of Clarence. Both were well-known figures of the day and it would have been natural at the time to name a road after the newly created Duke.

YORK WAY see COW LANE

STREET AND PLACE NAMES IN WATFORD

NOTES TO THE MAIN SEQUENCE OF STREET AND PLACE NAMES

1. The Rickmansworth Historian. No. 14. Autumn 1967. Page 353. C. J. M. Bradbury. Benskin's Watford Brewery 1867-1967.
2. James Stuart. Beechen Grove Baptist Church, Watford. Kingsgate Press, London and W. Michael & Son, Watford, 1907. Page 118.
3. Royal Commission on Historical Monuments (England). Inventory of Historical Monuments in Hertfordshire. H.M.S.O., 1910. Page 233.
4. Terry Coleman. The Railway Navvies. Hutchinson, 1965. Revised edition. Penguin, 1968. Page 80.
5. Watford Local Board of Health. Reports upon Complaints and Nuisances compiled by Unknown Officials of the Board between 1853 and 1856. (Manuscript entries). This Official was probably Thomas Redford (see Note 11 of the Introduction).
6. Roger Mortimer. The History of the Derby Stakes. Cassell, 1962. Pages 198-200.
7. E. J. Hobsbawm. Industry and Empire. Weidenfeld & Nicholson, 1968. Penguin, 1969. Diagram Appendix. Diagram No. 31—The British Ports in 1888.
8. Rudyard Kipling, from his poem entitled 'Recessional'.
9. Edmund Clerihew Bentley. His Poem entitled 'Lord Clive'.
10. Letter from the Agent of the Earl of Essex to the Directors of London & North-Western Railway dated 11th February 1857.
11. William Cobbett. Rural Rides. The Ride from Kensington to Worth in Sussex dated Monday, May 5th 1823 "... the town of Brighton in Sussex, 50 miles from the Wen, is on the sea-side, and is thought by the Stock-jobbers, to afford a *salubrious air*. It is so situated that a coach, which leaves it not very early in the morning, reaches London by noon; and, starting to go back in two hours and a half afterwards, reaches Brighton not very late at night. Great parcels of Stock-jobbers stay at Brighton with their women and children. They skip backward and forward on the coaches, and actually carry on stock-jobbing, in 'Change Alley', though they reside at Brighton".

APPENDIX 1 (Sections A, B and C)

This appendix should be consulted in conjunction with page 10 of the Introduction and the entry for Aynho Street in the main sequence of street and place names.

Appendix 1A has a list of plaques with scrolls and foliage, which are all clearly by Clifford and Gough. Appendix 1B lists plaques of a plainer style. Most of these by the evidence of style, naming and the architecture of the houses themselves are clearly by Clifford & Gough and are after 1868, the date at which the firm was founded. The reason that William Gough used certain names for his plaques is now obscure, although he worked on logical basic principles. In addition to straight-forward topographical names from North Oxfordshire, South Northamptonshire and Hertfordshire, many others were based on country houses in these areas and the families who lived in them. Furthermore if a family had more than one house, both names were sometimes used, even if one were outside the areas mentioned above. Also, if members of a family had married into the nobility elsewhere in the country, names in quite distant counties were used. This makes the whole matter incredibly complicated and I have not attempted to follow the tortuous trail to its end, as this would have demanded an almost completely new work in its own right. However, I have noted below some points of interest with the words in italics indicating names used in the plaques. The ownership of country houses is of course contemporary with the period William Gough was carrying out his building and often bears no resemblance to the situation today.

1. The Earl of *Jersey* owned Middleton Park, Oxfordshire and also Osterley Park, Middlesex, on the river *Brent*.
2. The *Langham* family lived at Cottesbrooke Hall, Northamptonshire.
3. The Clifton family of Gilsborough Grange, Northamptonshire, also owned *Lytham* Hall, Lancashire.
4. The Earls of *Radnor* owned Delapré Abbey (now the Northamptonshire County Record Office) and were related to the Earls of *Verulam* and *Rosebery*.
5. The Earl of Effingham of Tusmore House, Oxfordshire, was also related to the Earls of *Rosebery*.
6. Alexander William Hall of *Barton* Abbey, Oxfordshire was M.P. for Oxford from 1874 to 1880 and from 1885 to 1892.
7. The Marquis of Northampton of Castle *Ashby*, Northamptonshire also had a property at Torloisk, *Oban*, Argyllshire.
8. The Seat of the Marlboroughs was *Blenheim* Palace, Oxfordshire.

There remains as well a residue of rather general sounding names (such as Warren Place in Milton Street which can be tracked down to Warren Farm, just outside Aynho), the majority of which are likely to remain obscure unless some chance connection is discovered.

One plaque with scrolls and foliage and seven of the plainer style bear the initials E. C., clearly standing for Edwin Clifford and I have added these two letters at the end of the relevant entries. Edwin Clifford's son was named Herbert and in addition to Herbert Street this accounts for Herbert Terrace in Sutton Road and Bertie Terrace in Merton Road.

Also in Clifford Street there is a rectangular plaque with a large female figure

holding a scroll bearing the words 'Clifford Street'. This now has a rather forlorn, gap-toothed air, as some of the letters are missing. The female figure is of ample proportions and much more like a Victorian matron, or a Wagnerian soprano, than the Greek or Roman handmaiden that was presumably intended. It is altogether a charming, if somewhat provincial, tribute to the head of the firm.

In Pinner Road at the junction with the south side of Grover Road, there is just beneath roof level a small statue of Queen Victoria with the words 'Queens Terrace'. This is an equally charming and ample tribute to the then reigning monarch and is obviously the work of William Gough as it is associated with one of his plaques with scrolls and foliage.

Appendix 1C lists plaques which pre-date 1868 and are therefore clearly not the work of Clifford and Gough. The only other builders I have been able to discover who used plaques, was Andrew and Sons but I have not been able to identify any of them. Finally a group of cottages on the south side of the Rickmansworth Road near Cassiobridge Road bear a plaque dated 1890 and the monogram of the Earls of Essex.

In this appendix, I have taken 1914 as the great divide, and the reader will find none of the names such as Chez Nous, Dun Romin or Our Rome, which became so popular for individual houses after the First World War. I have however, included individual house names over porches and in the glass panels above front doors, if they are of sufficient character to merit inclusion and clearly pre-date 1914.

SECTION A

Aynho Street*	Harwood Terrace 1890
	Date on brickwork 1890
Banbury Street*	Lerwick Terrace 1892
	Date on brickwork also presumably 1892, although now partially obscured by pebble-dash
Clifford Street	Alexandra Terrace Barton Terrace* Brasenose Terrace*
	Morley Terrace
	Dates on brickwork 1888 and 1889
Derby Road	Colne View Terrace
Estcourt Road	Adelaide Villas 1892 Aynho Terrace 1880*
	Japanese Terrace 1868
Fearnley Street	Fearnley Terrace 1881 Jubilee Place 1887
	Tusmore Terrace 1881*
Franklin Road	Cambridge Terrace 1878
Grover Road	Banbury Terrace 1889* Rose Cottages 1892
	Dates on brickwork 1889 and 1890
Herbert Street	Codicote Terrace
	Dates on brickwork 1888 and 1889
Merton Road	Bertie Terrace 1881 (two of the same plaque)
Nascot Street	Calverley Cottages 1886
Oxford Street*	Charlton Terrace 1892*
	Dates on brickwork 1892 and 1893

Pinner Road	Queen's Terrace 1887
	Date on brickwork 1887
Queen's Road	Astrop House 1880* Banbury House 1880*
Souldern Street*	Danesbury Terrace 1891 Inverness Terrace 1891
	North Aston Terrace 1890* Oban Terrace 1891
	Dates on brickwork 1890 and 1891
Sutton Road	Herbert Terrace 1875 E.C.
Terrace Gardens	Nelson Place 1888
	Russell Place 1888 (two of the same plaque)
Upper Paddock Road	Clarendon Place 1891 Essex Place 1891
	Gordon Place 1889 Nelson Place 1891
	Russell Place 1891 Wolseley Place 1891
	- - - ley - - - 91 (the rest obscured by pebble-dash)
Victoria Road	Ebury Place 1892 Essex Place 1892
Villiers Road	Dulcet Villa 1882
Westland Road	Oxford Terrace 1878*
(formerly Weymouth	
Street North)	

SECTION B

Acme Road	Jersey Terrace 1896 Winifred Terrace 1899
Addiscombe Road	York Terrace
Balmoral Road	Quetta Villas Victoria Place 1901
Bradshaw Road	Rose Cottages
Brighton Road	Elgin Terrace (two of the same plaque, now almost invisible. Half of one plaque obliterated)
Buckingham Road	Date on brickwork 1909 (clearly Clifford and Gough by style)
Cardiff Road	Oxhey Cottage 1909
Cassio Road	Lomas House Conway 1901
	Mr. Gosling's Homes for Aged Women Founded 1896
Chalk Hill	Havelock Terrace Yewtree Villa
Church Road	Mormon Terrace (black paint on white brickwork now very faded) St. Andrew's Terrace
Clifton Road	Risingholm 1903
Cross Road	Crook Log Cottages 1901
Cross Street	Myrtle Terrace 1868
Denmark Street	Eastbourne Terrace 1883
Essex Road	Brent Cottage 1873 Eldercroft Fitzroy Villa (over porch) Verulam Villa 1884 (over porch) Les Villas du Jubilé Warwick Cottage 1873 or possibly 1875
Estcourt Road	Canada House Canada Terrace Estcourt Nursery 1868 Hope Cottage 1911 George V Place Prosper Cottage (over porch) Regent Terrace 1872 Ripley Cottages

	Souldern Cottages (one plaque 1869, the other 1870)*
	Souldern House 1870 (the present Clifford & Gough offices and yard)* Sydney Cottages 1870 Vernon House 1872
Garfield Street	Belgrave Place 1899 Garfield Place
	Garfield Terrace 1895 E.C. Lyndale Place 1898
	Raleigh Terrace 189- (the last digit was never cut) E.C.
	Rosebery Place 1899 Rutland Place 1898
Gartlet Road	Oxford Place 1882*
Gladstone Road	1903 Alexandra Place Arcot Villa (over porch)
	Cromer Villa (over porch) Deal House (over porch)
	The Ferns (over porch) Gladstone Villa (on glass over front door) Gloster House (over porch)
	Gordon Villa (over porch) Granville House (over porch)
	The Laurels (over porch) Nelson Villa (over porch)
	River view (over porch)
Grover Road	Lilla Cottage (plaque damaged)
Harwoods Road	Harwoods Terrace
Judge Street	Francis Terrace Harefield Terrace Natal Villas
Lammas Road	Essex Place 1891
Langley Road	Fern Cottages Lancaster House 1879
	Pleasant Place 1868
Leavesden Road	Braemar Terrace 1897 Longford Terrace 1896
	Ottawa Place 189- (the last digit was never cut)
Loates Lane	Cambridge Cottage Havana Cottages
	Manilla Cottages Pleasant Place 1873
Malden Road	Civel Cottage Pulford Terrace 1880 York Cottage
Milton Street	Dudley Place Hatton Place Ilsley Place 1900
	Baynard Place* Milton Villa 1897 Park Place
	Warren Place*
Nascot Street	Home Cottages 1870 Lorne Villas St. James's Villas 1883
Ottoman Terrace	Ottoman Terrace (painted on a metal plaque—very faded)
Oxford Street*	Margate Terrace 1893 E.C. Stockholm Terrace 1892 E.C.
Oxhey Avenue	Date on brickwork 1889 (clearly Clifford & Gough by style)
Park Road	Leonard Villas
Parker Street	Bellevue Place 1896 Claremont Cottages 1896
	Cromer Place Gresham Place 1897 Rosslyn Place 1894
Percy Road	Percy Villas
Pretoria Road	Pretoria Cottages 1901
Queen's Road	Ebenezer Cottages 1868 (now almost obliterated by mauve paint)
	Ebenezer House 1877 Laburnum Villas Rose Bank 1880
	Rose Cottages 1877 Victoria Cottages, Queen's Road 1873
	The Woodbines
Regent Street	Adowa Place 1894 Alford Place 1894 Blyth Place 1894
	Bradwell Cottages 1895 Brixton Place 1892

	Dalry Place 1894 Frinton Place 1892
	Fritwell Terrace 1894 E.C.* Grimsby Place 1892
	Langham Terrace 1893 Lodore Terrace 1894
	Malden Terrace 1894 E.C. Regent Terrace 1893 E.C.
	Reigate Terrace 1893 Swindon Place 1892
	Wembley Place 1892
	Date on brickwork 1893 (clearly Clifford and Gough by style)
Rosslyn Road	Kyleska
St. James' Road	Aston Villa (over porch) Malvern Villa (over porch)
	Mendip Villa (over porch) St. James Terrace
	Two square plaques dated 1897 with round medallions containing Queen Victoria's head and the following wording: 'Victoria 60 years Queen of Great Britain & Ireland, Empress of India.'
St. John's Road	Grove Villas
Salisbury Road	Ashby Terrace Recordia Terrace
Sandringham Road	Quainton Terrace 1908*
Shakespeare Street	Denby Place Lorne Place Malton Place Oriol Place
	Radnor Place
Sotheron Road	Belmont Cottage Ebury Cottages April 1869
	Hilldrop Cottages 1872 Phoenix Cottages 1874 W.W.
	? Cottages 1876 (plaque savaged and no longer recognisable)
Stamford Road	Myrtle Cottage 1869
Stanley Road	1902 Edward VII Place
Sussex Road	Eversleigh Glyndhurst Heath Villa 1901
	Milcombe Villa 1901* Also a plaque with an heraldic eagle above a castle
Sutton Road	Alma Terrace 1869 Crown Cottages 1873
	Cyprus Cottages 1878 W.H. (over porch)
	Fawn Cottage 1880 Hill Terrace
	King Street Cottage 1875 W.W. Myrtle Cottage 1875
	Oak Cottage 1876 Rose Cottages J.W. (date erased)
	Soho Villas (over porch) Vigo Villas (over porch)
	Woodland Cottage 1876 Wytham Terrace 1875*
Vicarage Road	Walsham Terrace
Victoria Road	Aldbury Terrace Blenheim Terrace* Elstead Place 1893
	Finchley Place 1892 Frances Place 1892
	Glencoe Place 1893 Linton Place 1894
	Lytham Place 1894 Octavia Place 1892
	Richmond Place 1892 St. Beetha's
Villiers Road	Cuba Cottages May Cottages 1881 Melbourne House
	Sydney House Virginia Cottages
Wiggenhall Road	Sylvanhay Villas
Windsor Road	Emmeline Terrace 1900
Woodford Road	Alpha Villas Arthur Cottages (demolished June 1972)

Woodford Villas (demolished)

	Woodford Villas (demolished)
	Milton Villas (painted on brickwork, almost obscured)
Yarmouth Road	Durban Villas 1899
York Road	Gordon Place 1891

SECTION C

Langley Road	E.B. Terrace 1867
Park Road	Frances Villas 1866
Queen's Road	Kintbury Cottage 1864
Stamford Road	Newton Cottage 1867
Villiers Road	Group of houses dated 1861 with the initials H.L.
	Memel Place 186? (plaque partially obscured with last digit indecipherable)
	Oxford Cottage (metal plaque, much faded. In spite of the name not Clifford and Gough, as by its position the cottage pre-dates 1868)
	The Pah (on glass above door) Rock Cottages 1866

*Names taken from within a fifteen mile radius of Aynho

APPENDIX 2

The following streets are named after Hertfordshire, Buckinghamshire and Bedfordshire villages.

Hertfordshire Villages	**Name of Street**
Aldbury	Aldbury Close
Bovingdon	Bovingdon Crescent
Bowmansgreen	Bowmans Green
Brent Pelham	
Furneaux Pelham	The Pelhams
Stocking Pelham	
Codicote	Codicote Drive
Cuffley	Cuffley Avenue
Felden	Felden Close
Gaddesden	Gaddesden Crescent
Kelshall	Kelshall
Kimpton	Kimpton Place
Redheath	Redheath Close
Westlea	Westlea Avenue (presumably also Eastlea Avenue and Leander Gardens by analogy)
Whitwell	Whitwell Road
Buckinghamshire Villages	
Ivinghoe	Ivinghoe Close
Jordans	Jordans Close
Bedfordshire Village	
Biddenham	Biddenham Turn (Part of Biddenham is in fact called Biddenham Turn)

APPENDIX 3

There is a Terrier of Watford dated 1798 and a Tithe Award dated 1842. This latter is accompanied by a fine series of 25″ maps dated 1844. From these it is possible to trace the following field names, which form the basis of street names. Cart Path Field appears on the 1844 Apportionment but it seems clear that the field was named after Cart Path and not vice versa. I have not here attempted to go into the meaning generally of field names as it is a vast and controversial subject in its own right. Readers who wish to pursue the matter further should consult A Dictionary of English Field Names by John Field. David and Charles, 1972.

Field Name	Farm Name	Street Name
1798 Lee Bushes	Lea Farm	Lea Bushes
1844 Lea Meadow		
1844 Cow Pasture	Lea Farm	Cow Lane
1798 Hillipers	Lea Farm	Phillipers
1798 Great Cran Hill	Kytes Farm	Cranfield Drive
Little Cran Hill		
1798 Grass Path Field	Garston Farm	Garsmouth Way
1844 Great Garsmouth		
Little Garsmouth		
1798 Great Gosmeres	Garston Farm	Gossamers
Little Gosmeres		
1798 First Field	Great Munden	First to Sixth Avenues
Second Field		(Fourth, Fifth and
Third Field		Sixth by analogy)
1798 Ganders Eye	Hare Farm	Ganders Ash
1844 Ganders Ash		
1798 Great Lemon Field	Hill Farm	Lemon Field Drive
1844 Great Lemon Field		
Little Lemon Field		
1798 Burry Bushes	Gammons Farm	Berry Avenue
1798 Hensey Downs	Wiggen Hall Farm	Nancy Downs
1844 Lower Hanseys		
Upper Hanseys		
Hansey Down Bottom		
Hansey Down Field		
1798 King's Field	Wiggen Hall Farm	Kingsfield Road
		Kingsfield Court

In addition to streets that can definitely be linked to field names in their own immediate area there remain others with a pleasing bucolic sound of a much more general kind. They may or may not correspond to actual topographical features, such as Butterwick meaning a dairy farm as an alternative for Lea Farm or Stud Green signifying that horses were actually bred in the area. It seems however, much more likely that the names listed on following page were a pleasant piece of nostalgia for a long-vanished agricultural past.

Butterwick	Farm Field	Linden Lea
Cross Mead	The Glebe	Long Barn Close
Fairfolds	Harvest End	Longcroft
Farmers Close	Heronslea	Stud Green

APPENDIX 4
Roads and Buildings named after Houses

Road or Building	Name of House	Street in which House was or is situated
Dellfield Close	Dellfield	Hempstead Road
Faircross House (Commercial Premises)	Faircross	The High Street
Farraline Road	Farraline	Wiggenhall Road
Grantchester Court	Grantchester	Clarendon Road
Hampden Way	Hampden	Ridge Lane
Haydon Road	Haydon Hill House (now a London Borough of Harrow Welfare Home)	Merry Hill Road
Herga Court	Herga	Stratford Road
Kildonan Close	Kildonan	Hempstead Road
Minerva Drive*	Minerva	Rickmansworth Road
Oaklands Court	Oaklands	Hempstead Road
Shrubbery (Multi-Storey Car Park)	The Shrubbery	The High Street
Silverdell	Silverdell	Nascot Wood Road
Stamford Road	Stamford Lodge	Park Road
Stanbury Avenue	Stanbury	Hempstead Road
Upton Road	Upton House	The High Street
Woodlands Parade	Woodlands	The High Street
Woodville Court	Woodville	Hempstead Road

*In the early 1920's George Bolton, Borough Librarian from 1919 to 1950, lived at Minerva, 163 Rickmansworth Road. During his period as Borough Librarian, he was frequently consulted on matters connected with local names.

APPENDIX 5

There follows a series of descriptions of Watford by various authorities from 1598 until the advent of the railway, and illustrates how heavily topographical writers tend to lean upon their predecessors. It is interesting to compare these accounts with that of the Superintending Inspector to the General Board of Health, who produced the first really factual and realistic account of the town. (See the Introduction in conjunction with note 7). Also the Watford entry in the main sequence of street and place names discusses the various suggestions put forward from time to time about the origin of the town's name.

WATFORDE or WATELINEFORDE for that the *Watteline-streete* crosseth the *Colne* nere this place, and so coasteth to old *Verlame* as is sayd before. John Norden. A description of Hartfordshire, 1598. Reprinted, 1903. Page 27.

Somewhat lower I saw *Watford* and *Rickemanesworth* two mercate townes: concerning which I have read nothing of greater antiquity than this, that king *Offa* liberally gave them unto St. Alban; as also *Caishobery* next unto *Watford*. In which place Sir *Richard Morisin* knight, a great learned man, and who had beene used in Embassages to the mightiest Princes, under king Henrie the Eighth and king Edward the Sixth began to build an house, which Sir *Charles* his sonne finally finished.
William Camden. Britannia. First published in 1583 in Latin. The above is from the 1610 edition in English. Page 415.

WATFORD is scituated upon the River Colne, about three miles distant from Rickmeresworth towards the North East, and was denominated from Wetford at the South end of the Town, it was anciently parcel of that large Revenue, which that great and magnificent King *Offa* so generously gave to the Monastery of St. Alban, and divers of his Royal Successors confirmed this noble Gift with the additions of many large Immunities and Priviledges; among whom King *Henry* I. Granted that the Abbots and their Successors should have a Market in this Town; and King *Edward* IIII. by Letters Patents dated at Doddington 1. of *November* 1469. 9 *Ed*.IIII. Granted to them two Fairs to be held in this Town for Victuals, and other things, to continue for five days, to wit, one to be held on *Monday* in the Morrow of the Holy Trinity, and to continue for two days then next following, and the other to be held on the day and the Morrow of the Decollation of St. *John* Baptist, with all the Liberties and Freedom belonging to the Fairs.
Sir Henry Chauncy. The Historical Antiquities of Hertfordshire. 1700. Page 482.

Watford, or as some will have it, *Wetford*, because it being situated upon the River *Coln*, had anciently a Ford at the South End of the Town; but Mr. *Norden* says, That it is a Contraction of *Watelineford*, so called, because *Watling street* crosseth the *Coln*, near this Place, and so passeth to *Old Verulam:* 'Tis a Market-Town and hath a Market weekly on Tuesday, well stored with Country Provisions and other Necessaries; and two Fairs on the Monday after *Trinity* Sunday, and two Days after, and on the Decollation of St. *John Baptist*.
Rev. Thomas Cox. Magna Britannia; or Topographical, Historical, Ecclesiastical, and Natural History of Hertfordshire. 1720. Page 1012.

WATFORD, is a Market Town, about seventeen Miles from *London*, in the Diocese of *London*, and Hundred of *Caishoe*, in the Road to *Berkamsted*. And stands upon the *Colne*, where it makes two Streams, which run separately to *Rickmersworth*. Hence it hath doubtless its Name; not from the Ford's being wet, for I never heard of a dry one. Whether it has a *Saxon* Derivation from the two Streams, I cannot determine. But without much Difficulty we may presume it contracted from *Watlingford*, being a Passage from *Rickmersworth* and that Country to *Watling-street*.
Nathaniel Salmon. The History of Hertfordshire. 1728. Page 104.

STREET AND PLACE NAMES IN WATFORD

A little to the east of this village (Cashiobury) is the town of WATFORD, which took its name from its situation on the Roman highway called Watling-street, that crosses the river Colne at a ford near the town. It is a long irregular place, and in winter is exceedingly dirty, particularly at the east end; but a road has been raised a considerable heighth above the ordinary level of the ground, whereby the waters are now confined within proper bounds. The church, which stands at a little distance from the town, is an old building, with side isles, two chapels, and a square tower.

Walter Harrison. A New and Universal History, Description and Survey of the Cities of London and Westminster, the Borough of Southwark, and their adjacent parts. 1776. Page 582.

About two miles farther west lies *Watford*, a genteel market-town, 14 miles from *London*, upon the *Colne*, where it hath two streams, which run separately to *Rickmersworth*. Several alms-houses belong to this town, and an handsome free-school, built in 1704, and finished 1709, by *Elizabeth Fuller*, widow; and in the church are several handsome monuments. The town is very long, having but one street; at the entrance of it stands *Townsend-house*, which is large and handsome, and belongs to *Arthur Greenwellers*, Esq. Upon the river is a large silk manufactory, which is three stories high, and has thirty-three sash windows on each side; it employs an hundred persons, and belongs to *Thomas Deacon*, Esq; who lives in the town.

'A Gentleman of Eminence in the literary World.' A Tour Through the Whole Island of Great Britain . . . (originally by Daniel Defoe) 8th edition. 1778. Volume 2. Pages 139 and 140. It seems unlikely that Defoe ever came to Watford himself, as the town was not mentioned in editions for which he was responsible.

WATFORD, Hertfordshire, is fourteen miles north-west from London, measured from Tyburn turnpike, eight south-east of St. Alban's, one mile north of Bushey, and three and a half east of Rickmersworth: is situated on a hill, whose elevation is about eighty or ninety feet. About midway up the town, on the left-hand-side of the road, stands the church, a large building of stone . . .

A little farther up the town than the church stands the market-place, a long square building. The market is on Tuesday, for corn, cows, sheep and hogs. There are two fairs in the year, one on the Tuesday after Trinity-Sunday, and the other on the 9th September; the latter is called the statute, and is for hiring of servants; but on both days toys are sold, &c. The principal manufactory of this town is throwing of silk, and for which there are three different buildings, two worked by horses and one by water. That which is worked by water is by far the largest. The river Coln runs at the back of Watford town, and through the bottom thereof; and, turning a little, may be seen from the houses on the other side of the town, and may be said in part to surround the town, in the vicinity of which it turns four mills, viz. a paper-mill belonging to Mr. Lewin, called Bushey-mill; a flour-mill in the town of Watford, occupied by Mr. Henry Field; the silk-mill, occupied by Mr. Paumier; and a paper-mill, occupied by Mr. Lepard, which is called Hamper-mill.

Universal British Directory . . . 1792. Vol. 4. Pages 697 and 701.

Watford is a large, populous, and busy town; the houses are principally of brick; many of them are respectable and handsome buildings; they principally range on the sides of the high road, and extend in a north-westerly direction rather more than a mile. The chief employment of the laboring classes is derived from agriculture; but additional labor is furnished by the *throwing of Silk*, three Silk Mills having been established in and near the town. The largest mill is worked by the waters of the Colne river; but the others are worked by horses. The population of Watford, as ascertained under the late Act, was 3530; the number of houses was 691.

Edward Wedlake Brayley and John Britton. The Beauties of England and Wales; or, original delineations, topographical, historical, and descriptive of each county. 1806. Vol. 7. Page 304.

WATFORD is situated upon the river Colne, about three miles distant from Rickmansworth towards the north-east, and was so called from Wet and Ford at the south end of the town, where was a ford over the Colne. It was part of the endowment of Offa to the monastery of St. Alban, and was by some supposed to have been Wallingford. Before the Conquest it was part of Cashio, and belonged to the abbey till the dissolution, when the stewardship of it was given to John Lord Russel, of Chenies, in Buckinghamshire. James I. granted it to the Lord Chancellor Egerton, Baron of Ellesmere, in whose descendants, the Dukes of Bridgewater, it remained till the year 1760, when the Earl of Essex purchased it, and it is now in his descendant, the present earl.

The praetorian or consular way made by the Romans in this county, called Watling-street, crosses the Colne near it, and passes on to Verulam, near St. Alban's. It consists of one very long street, which is extremely dirty during the winter, and the waters of the river at the entrance of the town are often so much swelled by the floods as to be impassable. Here are several alms-houses and other funds for the poor; a charity-school for forty boys, and a free-school built in 1704 by Mrs Elizabeth Fuller. The charter of the market was granted by Henry I., and Edward IV. gave them the liberty of two fairs annually. The market-house is a long building, supported on wooden pillars. The quantity of corn sold here is very great; the police of the town is under the neighbouring magistrates. Three silk-mills have lately been erected here. The population of Watford is estimated at 3530 inhabitants.

Henry Hunter. The history of London (Hertfordshire section) 1811. Pages 780-781.

The town of Watford is situated at the distance of fourteen miles from London, upon the high road leading from thence to Aylesbury in Buckinghamshire; and consists of one long street, rising with gentle slope from the river Colne. King Henry the Second granted to it a weekly market to be held on a Tuesday; and King Edward the Fourth two fairs, one to be kept on Trinity Monday and the two succeeding days, the other on the feast of St. John Baptist and the succeeding day.

Robert Clutterbuck. The History and Antiquities of the County of Hertford. 1815. Vol. 1. Page 236.

Watford is fifteen miles from London, and is situated on a smart eminence, gradually rising, and terminating with the end of the town . . . Watford is nearly a

mile in length: its entrance from London is very indifferent, though of late much improved. It is a populous and busy town, with a market on Tuesday, for corn straw, platt, etc. There are two fairs in the year, one on the Tuesday after Trinity Sunday, and the other on the 9th of September. The principal manufactory of this town is throwing of silk, and the paper mills in its neighbourhood employ many hands. The river Coln runs through the town, and has excellent fishing.
J. Hassell. Tour of the Grand Junction (Canal) ... 1819. Pages 14, 15.

WATFORD. The market-town of Watford, having a population, according to the last returns, of 3976, is 20½ miles W.S.W. from Hertford, and 14½ N.W. from London. The Abbots of St. Alban's had various privileges granted them for this manor, by different sovereigns: the charter of the market was bestowed by Henry the First; and Edward the Fourth gave them liberty to hold two fairs annually. The market-house is a long building, rough-cast above, and supported on wooden pillars beneath. The quantity of corn sold here is very great; and the number of sheep, cows, calves, hogs, &c. is proportionable.
The New British Traveller, or Modern Panorama of England and Wales (Hertfordshire section). 1819. Vol. 3. Page 56.

WATFORD is a neat town, consisting principally of one street rising with a gentle ascent nearly 1m.; about the centre stands the church, a spacious structure, with a massive embattled tower at the west end 90 feet high, surmounted by a spire: the interior is commodiously fitted up, and contains several elegant monuments, but particularly two of the Morison family, by Nicholas Stone. Agriculture, the manufacture of paper, and throwing of silk, form the chief employments of the inhabitants; for the purposes of the latter a mill has been erected near the town, which is worked by the waters of the Colne river. The market on Tuesday is well supplied with corn and cattle.
Paterson's Roads; being an entirely original and accurate description of all the direct and principal cross roads in England and Wales, with part of the roads of Scotland. 16th edition, by Edward Mogg. 1822. Page 172.

In those quiet old days—only a generation ago, yet separated by what a wide intellectual interval from this sixth decade of the century!—Watford was a most quiet little country town, exceedingly well-known by the four thousand people who dwelt there, but not very widely known to the rest of the world. It possessed the usual features and social elements of a small market-town in an agricultural district, with no staple trade or manufacture. There were the neighbouring nobility and gentry, who made their appearance on great occasions, as at public meetings, concerts, or county elections. There were triumphant Tories, and wistful Whigs. There was the vicar, an earl's nephew, generally to be seen on a fine day, with his portly figure, white trousers, and jovial face, chatting with his parishioners; or not seldom, in the hunting season, riding through the street (there was but one street), in his scarlet jacket and white cords. There was the dissenting minister who preached at the quaint little old Baptist chapel (since superseded by a modern structure), the secluded position of which, entrenched among crooked back-lanes, told of the

times in which Nonconformity had been fain to seek safety in obscurity. There were two or three rival lawyers, and two or three rival doctors, and two rival principal inns, one with a gentlemanly landlord, the other with an unparalleled waiter. There was the retired great bookseller, and the great brewer preparing to retire, and the great nobody, at the great white house, and the great man, who drove about in a little chaise, because he was too bulky to walk, never went to church because he could not get into his pew, and was credibly reported always to eat a leg of mutton as a precaution before he went out to dine. There were rich millers and farmers, and well-to-do shopkeepers, and hard-working cottagers, too many publicans, and a full average of beggars and scamps. There were electioneering squabbles (for the county), and great savings' bank questions, and great right-of-way questions; and, in later years, a great Reform banquet and illumination; and, as in most small country towns, where everybody knows everybody, a great deal of gossip. As the town lay several miles off the Great North Road, there was no great amount of traffic passing through. Two or three London coaches, on their way to Chesham, Hempstead, or some other town further down in the country, were the modest substitute for long railway trains, with their two or three hundred passengers. A few lumbering carriers' vans represented the "goods trains" of later and more impatient times. Every night, the mail-coach, with its flaring eyes and red-coated guard, made the quiet streets echo to its horn, picked up, perhaps, its one passenger, and excited mysterious feelings of respect and wonder in the minds of little boys. All around the dear, dull, quiet little town lay the still more quiet country. Two minutes would bring you into it; on the one side across the little river Colne, into green low-lying meadows, which the artificially-raised banks do not keep the stream from overflowing for miles after very heavy rains; on the other, through the lime-shaded churchyard, out among cornfields and homesteads, and shady lanes; or over stiles and through footpaths, to where the deer browse among the spreading limes and beeches, or hide in the thickets of tall fern, in Cassiobury Park. Eustace R. Conder. Josiah Conder: a memoir. 1857. Pages 239-241. Josiah Conder was a notable non-conformist writer and divine and lived at Watford Field House from 1824 to 1839. In this memoir his son Eustace describes Watford as he recalled it in the late 1820's.

Returning to the turnpike road, we reach at the distance of seven miles and a half from St. Alban's, the large, populous, and bustling town of WATFORD. Brick is in general the article employed in their construction, many of which are highly elegant, and are chiefly built along the side of the road.
The town is situated on a hill, whose elevation is about 80 or 90 feet. Part of the town extends beyond the foot of the hill, and through this part the river Colne runs, making a reach after it passes the houses, so as to pass by two sides of it.
The Colne adds much to the picturesque beauty of the surrounding scenery; on this river are several silk mills. Watford Canal commences near the town, where it unites with the grand junction canal, and runs to St. Alban's, passing in its course through the parishes of Watford, Bushey, Aldenham, and St. Peter's. The town contains 918 houses, and 4713 inhabitants.

STREET AND PLACE NAMES IN WATFORD

George Alexander Cooke. A Topographical and Statistical Description of the County of Hertford, 2nd edition. n.d. but c.1825. Pages 145, 146. This description shows signs of scissors, paste and imagination. Watford Canal was never built, although an Act to carry this out was published dated June 2nd 1795 (35 Geo.III, Chap. 85). It is also clear that a line or lines are missing at the beginning after the word WATFORD.

WATFORD, a parish in the hundred of *Cashio*, or liberty of St. *Albans*, county of *Hertford*, comprising the market town of Watford, and the hamlets of Cashio, Levesden, and Oxhey, and containing 4713 inhabitants, of which number, 2960 are in the town of Watford, 20 miles (W.S.W.) from Hertford, and 15 (N.W.) from London. This town, situated on the river Colne, derives its name from the Watling-street, which passes in the vicinity, and from a ford over the river, to which latter its origin also is attributed: it consists of one principal street, about a mile in length, is well built, paved, and supplied with water by a forcing pump, erected by subscription. By means of the Grand Junction canal, which passes a mile to the westward, a communication is maintained with the metropolis and the northern part of the kingdom. The manufacture of straw-plat, and three silk-throwsting mills, employ a considerable number of persons; there are likewise eight malt-kilns, and two extensive breweries. The market, granted by Henry I., is held on Tuesday: the market-house is an indifferent building supported on wooden pillars, with granaries over it, and its situation is very confined. Fairs are on the Tuesday after Whit-Tuesday, and on August 29th and 30th, for cattle and pedlary; the latter, originally granted by Edward IV., in 1469, had fallen into disuse, but was revived in 1827.
Samuel Lewis. A Topographical Dictionary of England . . . 1831. Vol. 4. Pages 407, 408.

WATFORD. It is situated on the river Colne, and consists of one principal street, well built and paved, and about a mile in length. The inhabitants are chiefly employed in three silk throwsting-mills, and the manufacture of straw plat; there are also malt-kilns, and extensive breweries. The market-house is a long building, supported on wooden pillars, with granaries above. The Grand Junction Canal passes about a mile west of the town, and the Birmingham Railway Station is close to the town.
Thomas Dugdale. Curiosities of Great Britain. n.d. but c.1841. Vol. 3. Pages 1518, 1519.

WATFORD is a market town and parish (including the hamlets of Cashio, Levesdon and Oxhey), in the hundred of Cashio, or liberty of St. Albans—15 miles N.W. from London, 20 W.S.W. from Hertford, about 7 S.S.W. from St. Albans, and 3 E. by N. from Rickmansworth; pleasantly situated on a gently rising eminence, upon the river Colne, over which there is a viaduct for the London and Birmingham Railway, which important line passes the town; and about a mile from it is a station, where a large hotel has been erected for the accommodation of passengers waiting for the trains. The Grand Junction canal passes a mile to the

west of the town; by the latter the transmission of its products and the introduction of those of other places is effected, and a water communication maintained with the metropolis and the northern counties. Watford consists of one main street, nearly a mile and a half in length, well lighted with gas from works established in 1834. The manufactures comprise silk, straw plat and paper; the malting business is extensive, and there are some corn-mills of great power and one for the manufacture of oil cake.

James Pigot. A Pocket Topography and Gazeteer of England (Hertfordshire section). 1842. Page 235.

BIBLIOGRAPHY

For the early development of the town, general county histories give a certain amount of background guidance. These are Sir Henry Chauncy's Historical Antiquities of Hertfordshire (London, 1700), Nathaniel Salmon's History of Hertfordshire (London, 1728), Robert Clutterbuck's The History and Antiquities of the County of Hertford . . . (3 vols. London, 1815-1827) and John Cussans' History of Hertfordshire (3 vols. London, 1870-1881, reprinted by EP Publishing Ltd., 1972). It is however not until the Report to the General Board of Health on a Preliminary Inquiry into the Sewerage, Drainage and Supply of Water and the Sanitary Conditions of the inhabitants of the Town of Watford by George Thomas Clark (London, H.M.S.O., 1849), that a really straightforward account becomes available. This invaluable view of Watford halfway through the nineteenth century is supplemented by a wealth of fascinating detail in Henry William's History of Watford and Trade Directory (London, 1884). A great deal of this is factual, but in some parts there is a tendency to tell a good story for its own sake rather than worry too much about strict historical accuracy.

For Watford, the relevant section of the Victoria County History of England is Volume 2 for Hertfordshire covering the Cashio Hundred, which is edited by William Page (Constable, 1908, reprinted by Dawsons, 1971), and as is typical of the series at that time, concentrates mainly on ecclesiastical matters, land tenure and the nobility and gentry, rather than social, educational and economic changes in the life of ordinary people. William Saunders, a local schoolmaster, produced a History of Watford (C. H. Peacock, 1931, reprinted by S.R. Publishers, 1970), which deals largely with the period up to the coming of the railway and concerns itself only briefly with the century that followed.

Although there still remains a great need for an up-to-date narrative history of the town for the period after 1850, there is a wealth of fascinating and essential detail in two pictorial histories, one by Robert Sayell, my predecessor in office, (Watford Borough Festival of Britain Committee, 1951) and the other by the Watford Camera Club (J. B. Nunn, 1963). My own Pictorial History (Watford Borough Council, 1972) concentrates exclusively on the period 1922-1972. The section on Watford in W. Branch Johnson's Industrial Archaeology of Hertfordshire (David & Charles, 1970) is a well-written and informative survey of a subject now of rapidly increasing interest.

Too little attention has been paid to the development of local government and the public utilities and the only real study has been an unpublished thesis on the Watford Local Board of Health for the period from 1850-1875 by Victor Hatley, Librarian of the Northampton College of Technology. This was written as part of a first degree at Durham University in 1953, but shows considerable maturity and is well documented.

The local newspapers, the Watford Observer (1863 to the present with a Centenary Supplement in 1963 and a Supplement to celebrate the Golden Jubilee of Watford as a Borough in 1972) and the Watford Post (1892-1970), both of which incorporated the words 'West Herts' in varying ways and at varying times, are mines of information, as also are the early general, special and water rate books. The sequences of all the latter are unfortunately broken, the general rate books being available for 1854, 1855, 1862, 1869, 1876, 1877, 1878, the special rate books for 1854 and 1856 and the water rate books for 1855-1871.

Although the Tithe Award of 1844 is accompanied by a series of 25″ maps of 1842, it is not until the 25″ Ordnance Survey maps of 1871 that the town really begins to take shape. Subsequent Ordnance Survey maps, especially the 6″ maps of 1897-1899, 1916-1925, 1934, 1940, the 25″ maps of 1897-1898, 1913-1914, 1934-1940 and the 50″ maps of 1959 show the spread of urban development in great detail. Land developers and estate agents produced prospectuses as land was sold for building and although they are mainly based on the work of the Ordnance Survey, they are also a valuable addition to it, as they give information about stillborn projects as well as those which succeeded.

Up to 1890, directory information is contained in general and Hertfordshire Directories. Pigot & Co.'s London & Provincial New Commercial Directory appeared in 1823/24 and its Royal National & Commercial Directory in 1839 while the Post Office Directory of London and 9 Counties was published in 1846. There followed Post Office Directories for Hertfordshire in 1851, 1855, 1859, 1866, 1874, 1878, 1882, 1890, 1895 and 1899. All these directories have short entries for Watford. For the period after 1890, there are two specifically Watford Directories. The first was published from 1890 to 1933 by C. H. Peacock, the Printer of the Watford Observer and the other has been produced from 1900 onwards by the national firm of Kelly's Directories. Peacock's Directory was an annual publication and Kelly's Directory was also an annual from 1900 to 1942. After that date it was issued in 1944, 1947, 1949, 1952, 1954, 1956, 1958, 1960, 1962, 1964 and 1966 when it reverted to an annual appearance. Both have accompanying maps, and streets often appear on them one or two years in advance of the directory information proper. This is of course useful when checking street names which were inspired by contemporary events, but directories of this kind are inevitably not always accurate and should be used in conjunction with all other available documentary evidence.

Watford in 1891 (Robinson, Son & Pike, 38 Duke Street, Brighton) and A Brief Account of Watford (C. H. Peacock, 1909) are useful guides to the general and commercial history of the town in the late Victorian and Edwardian periods, while The Civic Survey (Watford Borough Council, unpublished, 1933) gives a comprehensive view of the work of the Local Authority at that date. Municipal Watford

and Its Housing Scheme (Watford Urban District Council, 1920) describes the genesis of the Harebreaks Estate and gives details of other municipal undertakings and services.

Four specialist works should also be consulted. These are the Rev. James Stuart's Beechen Grove Baptist Church, Watford (London, Kingsgate Press and Watford, W. Michael & Son, 1907), W. G. Hughes and M. Sweeney's Watford Grammar Schools for Boys and Girls 1704-1954 (Watford Grammar School Governors, 1954), John Britton's History and Description . . . of Cassiobury Park (London, 1837) and Roderic Owen's Lepard & Smith Ltd., 1757-1957 (Lepard & Smith, 1957). All give valuable insights into important aspects of the town's history.

For early railway development in the area the basic works are Osborne's Guide to the Grand Junction . . . Railway (Birmingham and London, 1838). A Railroad Guide from London to Birmingham (London, 1839), Thomas Roscoe's London and Birmingham Railway (c1840) and its revision entitled An Illustrated History of the London & North Western Railway . . . (London, 1847). Terry Coleman's The Railway Navvies (Hutchinson, 1965, Penguin, 1968) is also helpful. Canal construction in the district is covered by J. Hassell's Tour of the Grand Junction . . . (London, 1819) and two books by Charles Hadfield, British Canals (David & Charles, 4th edition, 1969) and Canals of the East Midlands (including part of London), 2nd edition (David & Charles, 1970).

In dealing with biographical material, the various volumes of both the Dictionary of National Biography and Who was Who together with the local press are indispensable. In addition Eustace Conder's Josiah Conder—a Memoir (John Snow, 35 Paternoster Row, 1857), Miriam Leech's David Greenhill, Master Printer (published privately, 1950) and Mary Pownall Bromet's Response (Methuen, 1935) give specialist local information.

In trying to determine place names I have been guided largely by The Place-Names of Hertfordshire by J. E. B. Gover, Allen Mawer and F. M. Stenton (C.U.P., 1938), Eilert Ekwall's Concise Oxford Dictionary of English Place-Names (O.U.P., 4th edition, 1960), The Names of Towns and Cities in Britain by W. F. H. Nicolaisen, Margaret Gelling and Melville Richards (Batsford, 1970) and English Place Name Elements by A. H. Smith (2 vols., C.U.P., 1956). John Field's Dictionary of English Field Names (David & Charles, 1972) has also been of great assistance.

The two basic works for architectural matters are the Inventory of the Historical Monuments in Hertfordshire by the Royal Commission on Historical Monuments for England (H.M.S.O., 1910) and the Hertfordshire volume of the Buildings of England series by Sir Nikolaus Pevsner (Penguin, 1953). Amid a host of general and specialist books on architectural history I have found the following works to be illuminating and informative: Howard Colvin's Biographical Dictionary of English Architects 1660-1840 (John Murray, 1954), Rayner Banham's Guide to Modern Architecture (The Architectural Press, 1962), Henry-Russell Hitchcock's Architecture Nineteenth and Twentieth Centuries (Penguin-Pelican History of Art, 1958), The Encyclopaedia of Modern Architecture edited by Gerd Hatje (Thames & Hudson, 1963), Robert Furneaux Jordan's Victorian Architecture (Penguin,

1966), Victorian Architecture edited by Peter Ferriday (Cape, 1963), Sir Nikolaus Pevsner's An Outline of European Architecture (Penguin, 7th edition, 1963) and Pioneers of Modern Design (Penguin, 1960).

For background historical material R. C. K. Ensor's England 1870-1914 (O.U.P., 1936) has now been inevitably superseded in some respects by later works, but as it stands midway between the high Victorian noon and the present, it combines a reasonably modern approach with a not too great distance from its subject matter and gives many interesting insights into the working of the Victorian mind. I have therefore used it in conjunction with Asa Briggs' Victorian Cities (New ed., Penguin, 1968) and together both works have been invaluable in setting the scene in nineteenth century Watford. Finally, mention should be made of the periodical, The Rickmansworth Historian (Quarterly, Rickmansworth Historical Society, 1961 to date), which has a certain number of articles on Watford.

Reader's Personal Notes